Sew-No-More
HOME DECOR

Decorating your home has never been easier or more fun than it is today, thanks to some wonderful new products and techniques that save you time and money. Now, with the creative guidance you'll find in Sew-No-More Home Decor, you can have exactly the look you want — without sewing a single stitch or hiring an expensive decorator! As your own interior designer, you'll enjoy the convenience and ease of using fusible products and fabric glue to make items that have traditionally been sewn, like curtains, table runners, and even slipcovers.

Spend an afternoon with us and fashion a trio of coordinating pillows, take an evening to turn a simple sheet into a lovely shower curtain, or spend a day with us and transform an entire room — all for a fraction of what you'd pay at department stores or designer shops! Each of our eight fully coordinated collections features statement-making projects that establish the room's mood, along with smaller, quick-to-make accents to carry out the theme. You can even mix and match projects from different sections. Best of all, you don't have to be an experienced seamstress to pull off any of these great looks!

As you begin your new decorating adventure, keep in mind that choosing your fabrics is probably the most important consideration — their colors, textures, and designs set the mood for your decor. We chose versatile, readily available fabrics for our projects, and we've given you swatches at the beginning of each section to help you see how to select solids and prints that work well together. Now that you know how simple and quick it is to dress up a room, you can change your decor as often as you change your mind!

LEISURE ARTS, INC.
LITTLE ROCK, ARKANSAS

Sew-No-More
HOME DECOR

EDITORIAL STAFF

Editor-in-Chief: Anne Van Wagner Childs
Executive Director: Sandra Graham Case
Executive Editor: Susan Frantz Wiles
Publications Director: Carla Bentley
Creative Art Director: Gloria Bearden
Production Art Director: Melinda Stout

PRODUCTION
TECHNICAL
Managing Editor: Sherry Taylor O'Connor
Senior Editor: Kathy Rose Bradley
Senior Technical Writers: Kimberly J. Smith and
  Ann Brawner Turner
Technical Writers: Candice Treat Murphy and
  Emily Jane Barefoot

DESIGN
Design Director: Patricia Wallenfang Sowers
Senior Designer: Donna Waldrip Pittard
Designers: Linda Diehl Tiano, Rebecca Sunwall Werle,
  Diana Heien Suttle, and Risa Johnson
Design Assistant: Kathy Womack Jones

EDITORIAL
Associate Editor: Linda L. Trimble
Senior Editor: Laurie S. Rodwell
Senior Editorial Writer: Tammi Williamson-Bradley
Copy Editor: Laura Lee Stewart

ART
Book/Magazine Art Director: Diane M. Ghegan
Senior Production Artist: Michael A. Spigner
Production Artist: M. Katherine Yancey
Creative Art Assistant: Judith Howington Merritt
Typesetters: Cindy Lumpkin and Stephanie Cordero

ADVERTISING AND DIRECT MAIL
Associate Editor: Dorothy Latimer Johnson
Advertising and Direct Mail Copywriters: Steven M.
  Cooper, Marla Shivers, and Tena Kelley Vaughn
Designer: Rhonda H. Hestir
Art Director: Jeff Curtis
Production Artist: Linda Lovette Smart

BUSINESS STAFF

Publisher: Steve Patterson
Controller: Tom Siebenmorgen
Retail Sales Director: Richard Tignor
Retail Marketing Director: Pam Stebbins
Retail Customer Services Director: Margaret Sweetin
Marketing Manager: Russ Barnett

Executive Director of Marketing and Circulation:
  Guy A. Crossley
Fulfillment Manager: Byron L. Taylor
Print Production: Nancy Reddick Lister and
  Laura Lockhart

MEMORIES IN THE MAKING SERIES

Library of Congress Catalog Number 93-85971
International Standard Book Number 0-942237-33-1

TABLE OF CONTENTS

CLASSIC ELEGANCE

Page 6

COUNTRY WEST

Page 24

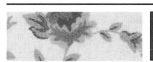 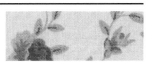

ROMANCING THE PAST

Page 36

TABLE OF CONTENTS

 FRENCH COUNTRY CHARM

Page 48

 ROSY HAVEN

Page 62

AMERICAN COUNTRY

Page 80

TABLE OF CONTENTS

 CASUAL MIX

Page 92

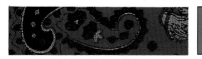 SPORTY RETREAT

Page 104

CLASSIC ELEGANCE

*T*imeless and traditional, this elegant collection has a classic look that will always remain in style. Fabrics in neutral colors and tone-on-tone combinations blend nicely with existing color schemes. Contrasting fabrics and patterns, such as moiré, brocade, and stripes, furnish visual interest, along with rich finishing touches such as fringe, tassels, braid, and other trimmings. The light and airy window treatment here is easy to achieve — sheer ivory fabric and taupe cord and tassels are simply draped around a wooden rod and gracefully puddled on the floor. An inexpensive decorator table is covered with an artfully arranged pouf skirt and a fringed table topper. Displayed on the table, fabric-covered picture frames enhance the room's decor. Whether you're relaxing with your family or entertaining friends, you will enjoy classic style in this comfortable living and dining area.

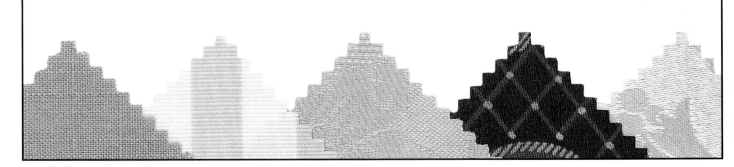

Swag and Cascade Window Treatment, page 22
Pouf Table Skirt with Fringed Table Topper, page 21
Fabric-Covered Picture Frames, page 23

*M*ade *of fabrics reflecting your dining room decor, table linens help provide a unified look. Our rich place mat (right) is edged with prairie points made by simply folding and gluing fabric squares. The napkin and napkin ring are easy to make, too, and a fabric wine glass coaster adds an elegant touch. Lending a distinctive air, the large and small topiary trees (below) are inexpensive to craft. Their fabric-covered pots are edged with gold trims, and the larger ones are enhanced by sponge painting and antiquing the rims.*

Table Setting, page 18
Topiary Trees with Fabric-Covered Pots, page 16

*A*ccents and accessories add as much appeal to a room as larger pieces do. A sponge-painted keepsake box (left) is dressed up with a padded fabric lid, gold trim, and tassels. For a striking window treatment, we selected fabric with a bold, symmetrical pattern to cover a roller window shade (below). Following the outline of the motif, we cut the shade away and added a gold tassel at the bottom. Covered with the same fabric, a lampshade makes a lovely coordinating accent.

Painted Box with Padded Lid, page 19
Fabric-Covered Window Shade, page 17
Covered Lampshade, page 17

9

Draperies with Swag Valance, page 20
Fringed Pillow, page 15
Pillow with Stenciled Bow, page 14
Envelope Pillow, page 15

*O*ur attractive window treatment (opposite) features graceful drapes fastened with elegant tiebacks and topped with two-tone swags. Scattered across a couch or clustered on a chair or love seat, throw pillows are a wonderful way to extend your decorating theme to every part of the room — and you're the only one who needs to know how easy they were to make!

Designed to coordinate with your decor, loose chair covers (left) are an ideal way to conceal mismatched or worn chairs. You can cover a group of chairs to arrange around the dining room table, or make just one for a delightful accent in the living room. Our cover is stenciled with pretty bows and features a fabric sash tied into a jaunty bow on the back of the chair (see page 13). We chose a variety of fabrics and trims to create our crazy-patch bench cover (below). To eliminate the need for lots of handwork, the fabric pieces are fused onto a length of muslin and the seams are covered with decorative braid.

Chair Cover with Stenciled Bows, page 12
Crazy-Patch Bench Cover, page 14

CHAIR COVER WITH STENCILED BOWS

(Shown on page 11)

For chair cover for a high-backed chair without arms, you will need a chair, approx. 5¹/₂ yds of 54"w to 60"w non-directional fabric (our chair is 43" high with a seat height of 17"; for a smaller or larger chair, adjust fabric amount), 1"w loop fringe, 1"w elastic, 1"w paper-backed fusible web tape, 1¹/₂" safety pins, masking tape, fabric glue, spring-type clothespins, removable fabric marking pen, an 8" square of acetate for stencil (available at craft or art supply stores), craft knife, cutting mat or a thick layer of newspapers, paper towels, removable tape (optional), stencil brush, fabric paint, and a black permanent felt-tip pen with fine point.

1. For top portion of chair cover (covering back and seat of chair), drape fabric piece over back of chair with selvages at sides of chair and 1 end of fabric extending just below chair seat at back of chair. Smooth fabric piece over back and seat of chair; trim fabric piece at front halfway between chair seat and floor. Set aside remaining fabric for skirt, sash, and bow.

2. Referring to **photo**, page 13, fold excess fabric at back of chair into pleats. Arrange pleats evenly and use safety pins to pin pleats in place below chair seat.

3. Measure around bottom of chair back; add 2". Cut a length of elastic the determined measurement. Overlapping ends of elastic at back, snugly wrap elastic around bottom of chair back to hold fabric in place; use a safety pin to secure elastic.

4. Gather 1 front corner of fabric around top of 1 front chair leg. Repeating Step 3, use elastic and a safety pin to secure fabric to chair leg. Repeat for remaining front corner of fabric. If necessary, trim excess fabric to 1" from floor.

5. For skirt, measure from edge of seat to floor; add 1" for top hem. (We used a linen-type fabric and left the fringed selvage edge unhemmed for the bottom edge of our skirt; if a bottom hem is desired, add 1" more to measurement.) Measuring width from 1 selvage edge of remaining fabric, cut a length of fabric the determined width and the entire length of the fabric. Measuring from remaining selvage edge, cut another length from fabric the determined width. Set aside center strip of fabric for sash and bow.

6. Make a 1" **single hem** along top long edge (not selvage edge) of each skirt fabric piece. If a bottom hem is desired, repeat for selvage edge.

7. (**Note:** Refer to **Fig. 1** for Step 7.) Place 1 skirt fabric piece right side up with selvage or hemmed bottom edge at bottom. Beginning 3" from left edge of fabric piece, press a 3" inverted pleat in fabric. Measure right edge of chair seat. Measure the determined length from first pleat in fabric and make two more 3" pleats. Measure front edge of chair seat. Measure the determined length from the third pleat in fabric and press remaining fabric to wrong side. Trim right edge of fabric piece 3" from pressed edge.

Fig. 1

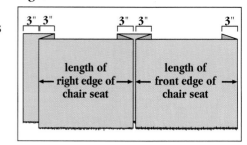

8. Referring to **Fig. 2**, repeat Step 7 for remaining skirt fabric piece, measuring left edge and back edge of chair seat.

Fig. 2

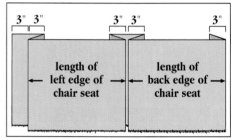

9. On right side of second skirt fabric piece, **fuse** web tape along left edge. With right sides up and matching raw edges, **fuse** right edge of first fabric piece to left edge of second fabric piece, forming another inverted pleat (**Fig. 3**).

Fig. 3

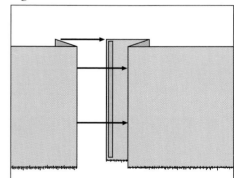

10. Using 3" lengths of web tape (use a 2" length in pleat formed in Step 9), **fuse** top edges of each pleat together to secure (**Fig. 4**). Use another 3" length to **fuse** top edge of fold together at right edge of skirt (**Fig. 5**).

Fig. 4

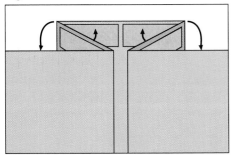

Fig. 5

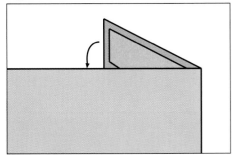

11. Measure top edge of skirt. Cut a length of loop fringe the determined measurement. Beginning ¹/₂" before first pleat in skirt, glue fringe along top edge of skirt. At right edge, trim fringe to ¹/₂" beyond edge of skirt; glue end to wrong side of skirt. Use clothespins to secure fringe until glue is dry.

12. Beginning with first pleat at right rear chair leg, use straight pins to pin skirt to top portion of cover, making sure bottom edge hangs evenly.

13. For stenciled bows, follow Step 1 of **Stenciling** to make stencil. Place stencil on cover and use fabric marking pen to lightly mark desired placement of each stenciled design on cover.

14. Place a length of masking tape on cover across top of chair back to simplify repositioning cover after stenciling. Unpin skirt from top portion of chair cover, remove elastic, and carefully lift remainder of cover off of chair.

15. Referring to markings on cover to position stencil, **stencil** each bow design on cover. Use black pen to outline each design and add detail lines as desired.

16. Using masking tape as a guide, reposition top portion of chair cover on chair; remove tape. Reposition elastic around chair back and around each front leg. Glue top edge of skirt in place along edge of seat and glue raw edges at opening of skirt together to form last inverted pleat. Use straight pins to secure skirt until glue is dry.

17. For sash and bow, trim remaining fabric strip to 12"w. Make a 1" **single hem** along each long edge of fabric strip.

18. With center of sash at front of chair back, wrap sash around chair back, covering elastic. Referring to **Figs. 6** and 7, tie ends of sash into a loose square knot at back of chair. Referring to **photo**, this page, tuck ends of sash into knot to form loops of bow; if bow loops are too long, trim ends of sash as needed. Use safety pins to secure ends of sash.

Fig. 6

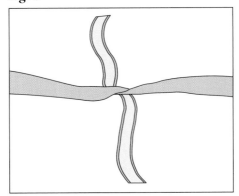

Fig. 7

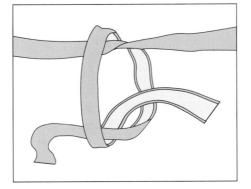

19. Cut a 4" x 8" strip from remaining fabric. Make a 1" **single hem** along each long edge of strip. Wrap strip around center front of sash, catching elastic in strip. Overlap ends of strip behind sash and use a safety pin to secure.

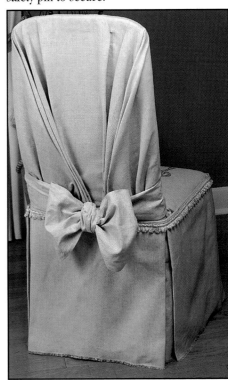

PILLOW WITH STENCILED BOW (Shown on page 10)

For an approx. 15" dia. pillow, you will need a 50" square and a 9" circle of fabric, two strong rubber bands, an 8" circle of lightweight cardboard for appliqué pattern, fusible interfacing, a 15" round pillow form, polyester fiberfill (optional), an 8" square of acetate for stencil (available at craft or art supply stores), craft knife, cutting mat or a thick layer of newspapers, paper towels, removable tape (optional), stencil brush, fabric paint, black permanent felt-tip pen with fine point, and fabric glue.

1. At center on wrong side of fabric square, gather an approx. 2" long bunch of fabric; wrap 1 rubber band tightly around bunched fabric (**Fig. 1**).

Fig. 1

2. Center pillow form on wrong side of fabric piece over bunched fabric.
3. Wrap fabric around form, gathering edges at center of form and distributing gathers evenly. If desired, stuff loose fiberfill into fabric around form for extra fullness. Wrap remaining rubber band tightly around gathered fabric close to form.

4. Trim excess fabric approx. 10" from rubber band. Open fabric above rubber band and tuck edges of fabric into hole at center, forming a "rosette" on back of pillow (**Fig. 2**). If necessary, glue fabric over rubber band and into opening at center to secure.

Fig. 2

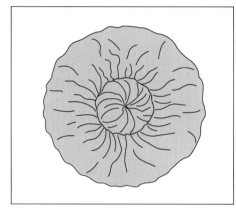

5. For stenciled appliqué, place fabric circle wrong side up on ironing board; center cardboard circle on fabric circle. At 1/2" intervals, clip edge of fabric to 1/8" from cardboard circle. Press clipped edges of fabric circle over edge of cardboard. Remove cardboard and press fabric circle again.
6. Draw around cardboard circle on interfacing. Cutting 1/4" inside drawn line, cut out circle. Center and **fuse** interfacing to wrong side of fabric circle, covering clipped edges of fabric.
7. **Stencil** bow design at center of right side of fabric circle. Use pen to outline design and add detail lines as desired.
8. Center appliqué on front of pillow. Leaving a 3" opening, glue edge of appliqué to pillow. Stuff a small amount of fiberfill under appliqué. Glue opening closed.

The projects on these pages require the use of the following techniques which are shown in **bold print** in the instructions. Please familiarize yourself with the General Instructions, pages 118 - 127, and these specific techniques before beginning the projects.

- *Fusing (page 123)*
- *Piecing Fabric Strips (page 123)*
- *Making a Single Hem (page 124)*
- *Making Binding (page 125)*
- *Stenciling (page 127)*

CRAZY-PATCH BENCH COVER
(Shown on page 11)

You will need a bench with padded seat, muslin, fabric scraps to cover seat, desired trims, paper-backed fusible web, fabric glue, liquid fray preventative, hot glue gun, and glue sticks.

1. Remove seat from bench. Cut a piece of muslin large enough to wrap around padding of seat and overlap 2" onto bottom.
2. **Fuse** web to wrong sides of fabric scraps. Cut scraps into desired shapes; remove paper backing. Beginning at center of muslin and overlapping edges of fabric pieces slightly, **fuse** pieces to muslin, trimming as necessary.
3. Beginning at center of covered muslin, use fabric glue to glue trims over raw edges of fabric pieces. Apply fray preventative to any exposed ends of trims.
4. Center seat upside down on wrong side of covered muslin. Alternating sides and pulling fabric until smooth, hot glue edges of muslin to bottom of seat.
5. Replace seat on bench.

ENVELOPE PILLOW (Shown on page 10)

For a 19" x 13" pillow, you will need a 19" x 13" fabric piece for pillow front, a 19" x 21" fabric piece for pillow back and flap, a $3^1/8$" x $2^1/4$ yd fabric strip for binding (see **Piecing Fabric Strips**), $3/4$ yd of $1^1/2$"w loop fringe, 2 yds of $1/2$"w gimp trim, 15" of $3/8$" dia. twisted cord, a $4^1/2$" long tassel, $3/4$"w paper-backed fusible web tape, polyester fiberfill, fabric glue, spring-type clothespins, and liquid fray preventative.

1. For flap on pillow back fabric piece, refer to **Fig. 1** and cut a point at 1 short edge (top).

Fig. 1

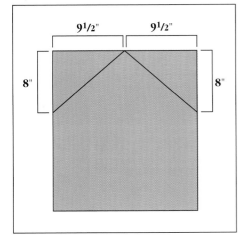

2. On wrong side of pillow front fabric piece, **fuse** web tape along each short edge and 1 long edge (bottom). Remove paper backing. Matching side and bottom edges, place pillow front and pillow back wrong sides together. **Fuse** pieces together along side and bottom edges.

3. For binding, follow Step 1 of **Making Binding** to make binding from fabric strip. Cut a 19" length, a $26^1/2$" length, and a $27^1/4$" length from binding.

4. Make a $3/4$" **single hem** at 1 end of $26^1/2$" binding length and at both ends of $27^1/4$" binding length.

5. Follow Steps 2 and 3 of **Making Binding** to complete each binding length.

6. (**Note:** In remaining steps, use clothespins to secure glued trims until glue is dry.) Insert bottom edge of pillow into fold of 19" binding length; **fuse** in place. Beginning with pressed end at 1 bottom corner of pillow and mitering binding at side corner of flap, repeat to apply $26^1/2$" binding length to 1 side edge of pillow and flap; if necessary, trim unhemmed end at point of flap. Repeat to apply remaining binding length to remaining side edge of pillow and flap. Use glue to secure mitered corners.

7. Press flap over pillow front. For trim on pillow, glue loop fringe along edge of flap, trimming to fit. Glue gimp over top edge of fringe and over inner edge of binding around pillow front. Apply fray preventative to ends of trims.

8. (**Note:** To prevent ends of cord from fraying after cutting, apply fabric glue to $1/2$" of cord around area to be cut, allow to dry, and then cut.) For tassel decoration, coil cord into a 2" dia. circle, gluing to secure. Glue hanging loop of tassel to back of coil. Glue decoration to flap of pillow.

9. Stuff pillow lightly with fiberfill. Glue flap closed.

FRINGED PILLOW

(Shown on page 10)

For an approx. 15" square pillow, you will need two $16^1/2$" fabric squares, 2 yds of 1"w brushed fringe, fabric glue, polyester fiberfill, and spring-type clothespins.

1. (**Note:** When gluing, use clothespins to secure fabric or fringe until glue is dry.) Press edges of both fabric squares $3/4$" to wrong side. Glue corners in place.

2. With fringe extending 1" beyond edge of fabric square, use a generous amount of glue to glue bound edge of fringe along pressed edge on wrong side of 1 fabric square.

3. Place fabric squares wrong sides together. Leaving an opening for stuffing, glue edge of remaining fabric square to bound edge of fringe.

4. Stuff pillow with fiberfill and glue opening closed.

TOPIARY TREES WITH FABRIC-COVERED POTS (Shown on page 8)

For each fabric-covered pot, you will need desired size round clay pot (we used 4$\frac{1}{2}$"h and 5$\frac{3}{4}$"h pots), fabric, desired trims (we used $\frac{7}{8}$"w loop fringe, $\frac{1}{2}$"w gimp trim, $\frac{3}{8}$"w gold metallic trim, and $\frac{1}{4}$" dia. twisted cord), hot glue gun, and glue sticks.
For each large pot, you will **also** need peach, light tan, dark brown, and metallic gold acrylic paint; black waterbase stain; plastic or coated paper plates; foam brushes; small sponge pieces; a soft cloth; matte clear acrylic spray; tracing paper; and removable tape.
For each topiary tree, you will need desired size plastic foam ball(s) or cone (we used 4", 5", and 6" balls and 9"h and 12"h cones), floral foam to fit in pot, twigs for trunks (we used birch twigs), sheet moss, sphagnum moss (optional), items to decorate trees (we used $\frac{1}{8}$" dia. bead garland, $\frac{1}{8}$" dia. twisted cord, a 24" long chair tie with tassels, $\frac{3}{4}$"w gold star floral picks, and 1$\frac{1}{2}$"w wired ribbon), hot glue gun, and glue sticks.

SMALL FABRIC-COVERED POT

1. Measure sides and bottom of pot (**Fig. 1**); add 3". Cut a fabric square the determined measurement.

Fig. 1

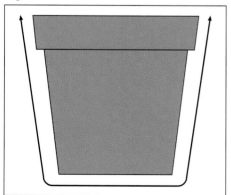

2. Place fabric square wrong side up. Center pot on square. Bring center of each edge of square over top edge of pot and glue to inside of pot. For pleats, bring corners of square over top edge of pot, adjusting pleats evenly; glue corners to inside of pot.
3. Glue desired trims to pot.

LARGE FABRIC-COVERED POT

1. Paint top half of inside and outside of pot peach; allow to dry. Swirl equal amounts of light tan and dark brown paint on plate; use a damp sponge piece to lightly stamp paint mixture over peach paint on pot; allow to dry. Stamp gold paint on pot.
2. Allowing to dry between coats, apply 2 coats of clear acrylic spray to painted areas of pot.
3. Apply stain to painted areas; remove excess with soft cloth and allow to dry.
4. Repeat Step 2.
5. To make pattern for fabric-covered area of pot, use a pencil and ruler to draw a straight line around pot approx. $\frac{1}{4}$" below rim for top edge of fabric; draw a vertical line from first line to bottom of pot (**Fig. 2**).

Fig. 2

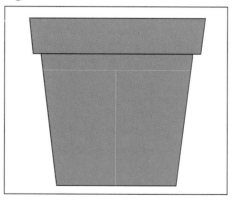

6. Place pot upside down. Tape 1 corner of a large piece of tracing paper at intersection of drawn lines (**Fig. 3**). Wrap tracing paper around pot, trimming bottom edge of paper just above rim of pot and trimming top edge of paper so paper lies flat against side of pot. Tape remaining edge in place.

Fig. 3

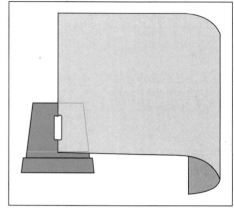

7. Trace bottom edge of pot and both pencil lines on pot onto tracing paper. For overlap on pattern, draw a vertical line on tracing paper $\frac{1}{2}$" to the right of vertical pencil line traced from pot (**Fig. 4**).

Fig. 4

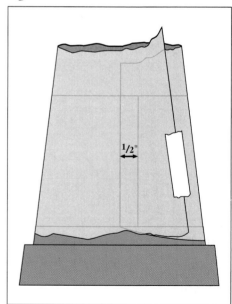

1/2"

8. Remove tape from overlapping edge of tracing paper. Leaving first edge of tracing paper taped to pot, unwrap tracing paper and finish tracing lines along bottom of pot and along pencil line around pot.

9. Remove tracing paper from pot and cut out pattern along outer pencil lines, including line for overlap.

10. Use pattern to cut a piece from fabric. Press 1 straight edge of fabric (overlap edge) 1/4" to wrong side. With remaining straight edge of fabric piece along vertical pencil line on pot, glue fabric piece around pot.

11. Glue desired trim(s) along top and bottom edges of fabric, covering raw edges.

TOPIARY TREE

1. Glue floral foam in pot to within 1/2" of rim. Glue sheet or sphagnum moss over foam, covering foam completely.

2. For trunk, cut twig to 4" longer than desired finished height of trunk. Insert 1 end of twig 2" into foam ball or cone; insert remaining end 2" into floral foam in pot. For double topiary, repeat to add a second ball at top of first ball.

3. Glue sheet moss over foam ball(s) or cone, covering form(s) completely.

4. Decorate tree as desired.

FABRIC-COVERED WINDOW SHADE (Shown on page 9)

You will need a roller window shade, fabric with a symmetrical pattern across width, 1/4" dia. twisted cord, a 5 1/2" long tassel, paper-backed fusible web, fabric glue, liquid fray preventative, permanent felt-tip pen, removable fabric marking pen, and spring-type clothespins.

1. If necessary, trim shade to fit window.

2. Cut slat casing from bottom of shade and discard. Unroll shade completely and use permanent pen to mark center top and center bottom of shade.

3. Lay shade right side up on right side of fabric. With shade centered over symmetrical design and center bottom of shade positioned at desired center bottom of fabric piece, use fabric marking pen to mark corners of shade on fabric. Use a yardstick to draw lines to connect corners. Cutting 2" outside drawn lines, cut out fabric piece.

4. Fuse web to wrong side of fabric piece. Trim top edge of fabric piece along top drawn line.

5. Lay shade right side up. With top edge of fabric next to roller, center fabric right side up over shade. Beginning at center of shade, **fuse** fabric piece to shade. Turn shade over and, if necessary, use a pin to pierce air bubbles on back of shade; press shade again on right side to **fuse** areas with air bubbles.

6. Carefully trim fabric even with side edges of shade.

7. For bottom edge of shade, begin at center bottom of shade and use fabric marking pen to draw a line upward from center toward 1 side edge of shade, using fabric design as a guide. Repeat to draw a symmetrical line from center bottom of shade to remaining side edge of shade. Carefully cut along drawn lines.

8. Apply fray preventative to side and bottom edges of fabric on shade.

9. (**Note:** To prevent ends of cord from fraying after cutting, apply fabric glue to 1/2" of cord around area to be cut, allow to dry, and then cut.) Glue cord along bottom edge on front of shade. Glue hanging loop of tassel to back of shade at center bottom. Use clothespins to secure cord and tassel until glue is dry.

10. Hang shade.

COVERED LAMPSHADE

(Shown on page 9)

You will need a lampshade, tissue paper, fabric, desired trims, spray paint (optional), spray adhesive, removable tape, fabric glue, and spring-type clothespins.

1. If desired, spray paint inside of lampshade; allow to dry.

2. Cover lampshade with fabric.

3. Measure around top edge of shade; cut lengths of trims the determined measurement. Beginning at seamline, glue trims over top edge of fabric; secure with clothespins until glue is dry. Repeat for bottom edge of shade.

> *The projects on these pages require the use of the following techniques which are shown in **bold print** in the instructions. Please familiarize yourself with the General Instructions, pages 118 - 127, and these specific techniques before beginning the projects.*
>
> • *Fusing (page 123)*
> • *Covering Lampshade with Fabric (page 127)*

For each place mat, you will need one 12" x 18" fabric piece for place mat top, one 12" x 17½" fabric piece for place mat backing, 2 fabrics for prairie points, lightweight fusible interfacing (optional; used if prairie point fabrics are lightweight), ½"w single-fold bias tape to match backing fabric, 2 yds each of desired trims (we used ½"w loop fringe, ¾"w gold metallic trim, and ½"w gimp trim), paper-backed fusible web, fabric glue, spring-type clothespins, and liquid fray preventative.

For each napkin, you will need a 19" fabric square and ½"w paper-backed fusible web tape.

For each napkin ring, you will need 9" of ⅜" dia. twisted cord, 11" of ³⁄₁₆" dia. twisted cord, a 3" long tassel, 2" of ¾"w fringe, 2" of ⅜"w trim, fabric glue, spring-type clothespins, hot glue gun, and glue sticks.

For a wine glass coaster to fit glass with up to 2½" dia. base, you will need three 5" fabric squares (we used rubber-backed tablecloth fabric for 1 square for coaster bottom), 10½" of ½"w single-fold bias tape to match bottom fabric, desired trims (we used 10" of ½"w loop fringe and 10" of ½"w gimp trim), fabric glue, liquid fray preventative, tracing paper, compass, and spring-type clothespins.

*The projects on these pages require the use of the following techniques which are shown in **bold print** in the instructions. Please familiarize yourself with the General Instructions, pages 118 - 127, and these specific techniques before beginning the projects.*

- *Fusing (page 123)*
- *Making a Single Hem (page 124)*

PLACE MAT

1. For place mat, **fuse** web to wrong side of place mat backing fabric piece. Remove paper backing. Matching wrong sides and long edges, **fuse** backing piece to center of top fabric piece.

2. (**Note:** Follow Step 2 to make 6 prairie points from 1 fabric and 4 prairie points from remaining fabric. For lightweight fabrics, **fuse** interfacing to wrong side of fabric before cutting squares for prairie points.) For each prairie point, cut a 4" square from fabric. Press square in half from top to bottom; press each top corner diagonally to meet raw edges (**Fig. 1**). Use glue to tack corners in place.

Fig. 1

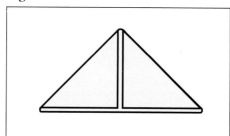

3. (**Note:** When gluing, secure fabrics or trims with clothespins until glue is dry. Follow Step 3 for each side edge of place mat.) Position place mat, 3 prairie points from 1 fabric, and 2 prairie points from remaining fabric wrong side up. Matching bottom edge of each prairie point to side edge of backing fabric, glue 3 same color prairie points along side edge of place mat (**Fig. 2**). Glue remaining 2 prairie points over first 3 prairie points (**Fig. 3**). Cut a 12" length of bias tape; center and glue bias tape over raw edges of prairie points.

Fig. 2

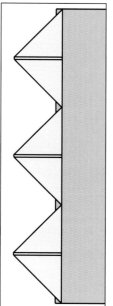

Fig. 3

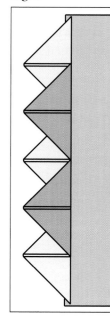

4. Cut two 19" lengths of bias tape. Press ends of each length ½" to wrong side; press each length in half lengthwise with raw edges to inside. Insert each long raw edge of place mat into fold of 1 length of bias tape and glue in place.

5. Glue trims along edge on right side of place mat, trimming to fit. Apply fray preventative to ends of trims.

NAPKIN

Make a ½" **single hem** along each edge of fabric square.

NAPKIN RING

1. (**Note:** To prevent ends of cord from fraying after cutting, apply fabric glue to ½" of cord around area to be cut, allow to dry, and then cut.) Hot glue ends of ⅜" dia. cord together.

2. (**Note:** When gluing trims, secure with clothespins until glue is dry.) Use fabric glue to glue fringe and then trim around top of tassel. Knot hanging loop of tassel $1/2$" above top of tassel; trim hanging loop above knot. Thread $3/16$" dia. cord through hanging loop. Use fabric glue to glue knot of hanging loop at center of cord.

3. Tucking ends under and using fabric glue to glue cord in place, wrap $3/16$" dia. cord around seam in cord ring, covering $3/4$" of cord ring.

WINE GLASS COASTER

1. For patterns, draw two 3" dia. circles on tracing paper; cut out. Fold 1 circle in half and unfold; cut $1/8$" from fold (**Fig. 4**). Discard large part of circle.

Fig. 4

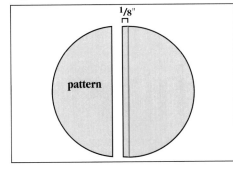

2. For coaster bottom, use circle pattern to cut a circle from 1 fabric square.

3. (**Note:** When gluing, secure fabrics or trims with clothespins until glue is dry.) For coaster top, press each remaining fabric square in half diagonally. Place straight edge of half circle pattern along pressed edge of each fabric square and cut out, forming 2 folded half circles. Glue raw edges of each half circle together.

4. Matching raw edges, place top pieces on right side of bottom piece. Glue pieces together along raw edges only.

5. Press 1 end of bias tape $1/2$" to wrong side; press bias tape in half lengthwise with raw edges to inside. Beginning with unpressed end, insert raw edges of coaster into fold of bias tape; glue in place.

6. Glue trims along edge on right side of coaster, trimming to fit. Apply fray preventative to ends of trims.

PAINTED BOX WITH PADDED LID (Shown on page 9)

You will need a wooden box with lid (ours measures $6^1/4$"w x $6^1/4$"l x $2^1/2$"h); peach, light tan, dark brown, and metallic gold acrylic paint; black waterbase stain; matte clear acrylic spray; foam brushes; small sponge pieces; a soft cloth; old toothbrush; plastic or coated paper plates; medium weight cardboard; fabric; polyester bonded batting; $1/2$"w gimp trim; 3" of $5/8$"w loop fringe; 7" of $1/8$" dia. twisted cord; two $1^1/2$" lengths of 1"w fringe and two $1^1/2$" lengths of $3/8$"w gimp trim for tassels; 10mm pearl half-bead; fabric glue; spring-type clothespins; hot glue gun; and glue sticks.

1. Paint box peach; allow to dry. Swirl equal amounts of light tan and dark brown paint on plate. Use a damp sponge piece to lightly stamp paint mixture on box; allow to dry. Stamp gold paint on box.

2. Allowing to dry between coats, apply 2 coats of clear acrylic spray to box.

3. Apply stain to box; remove excess with soft cloth and allow to dry. Dip toothbrush in stain and drag thumb across toothbrush to lightly spatter dots of stain on box; allow to dry.

4. Repeat Step 2.

5. For padded lid, cut a piece of cardboard same size as desired size of padding. Cut 2 pieces of batting same size as cardboard. Cut fabric 2" larger on all sides than cardboard.

6. Center both layers of batting, then cardboard, on wrong side of fabric. Alternating sides and pulling fabric until smooth, hot glue edges of fabric to back of cardboard.

7. Hot glue padded shape to lid.

8. Hot glue gimp along edge of padded shape.

9. (**Note:** Use fabric glue for Step 9. Use clothespins to secure trims until glue is dry.) For flower and tassel decoration, overlap ends of loop fringe and form fringe into a circle with straight edge gathered at center (**Fig. 1**); glue to secure. Coil center of cord as shown in **Fig. 2**; glue to secure. Glue coil of cord at center of loop fringe flower. For each tassel, wrap and glue 1 length of fringe around each end of cord with fringe extending beyond end of cord; glue 1 length of gimp around top of fringe.

Fig. 1

Fig. 2

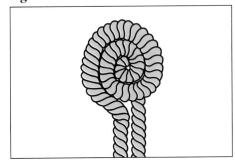

10. Hot glue half-bead to center of coil. Hot glue decoration to box.

DRAPERIES WITH SWAG VALANCE (Shown on page 10)

You will need a conventional curtain rod for draperies, a 4¼"w Continental® curtain rod for valance, fabric for draperies, fabric for tiebacks, 2 contrasting fabrics for valance, 1"w paper-backed fusible web tape, 2 decorative drapery tiebacks with tassels, four 1" safety pins, and 2 cup hooks.

DRAPERIES

1. Mount conventional rod.

2. To determine width of fabric panels, measure length of rod; multiply measurement by 1¼. To determine length of fabric panels, measure from top of rod to desired length; add 11¼" for casing and hem. Cut 2 panels from fabric the determined measurements, **piecing fabric panels** as necessary.

3. For each panel, make a 1" **single hem** along 1 short edge (top) of fabric length. Make a 1" **double hem** along each side edge of fabric length. Make a 4" **double hem** along bottom edge of fabric length.

4. For casing at top of each panel, **fuse** web tape along top edge on wrong side of panel. Do not remove paper backing. Press edge 2¼" to wrong side. Unfold edge and remove paper backing; refold edge and **fuse** in place.

5. Remove rod from window and insert through casing of each panel. Adjust gathers evenly across rod. Hang draperies.

6. For tiebacks, drape a tape measure around 1 panel in desired position; add 1" to measurement. Cut two 5"w fabric strips the determined measurement.

7. Make a 1"w **single hem** along each long edge of each fabric strip.

8. Drape 1 tieback around 1 panel, arranging pleats in panel as desired. Overlap tieback ends 1" and use a safety pin to secure at back of drapery. Tie 1 decorative drapery tieback around fabric tieback. Use a safety pin to secure

decorative tieback to fabric tieback at knot. Use cup hook to secure knot of tieback to wall. Repeat for remaining tieback.

VALANCE

1. Mount Continental® rod.

2. To determine width of each swag, measure length of rod; multiply measurement by 2½ and divide measurement by 4. To determine length of each swag, divide length of rod by 4; measuring from 1 end of rod, use a piece of tape to mark rod at the determined measurement. With 1 end of tape measure at end of rod and remaining end at tape mark, drape tape measure over rod. Adjust tape measure to desired length of swag (see **Diagram**, page 21); make a note of measurement on tape measure and add 2". Cut 2 pieces of each contrasting fabric the determined measurements.

3. (**Note:** Follow Steps 3 - 6 to make each swag, using 1 piece of each fabric for each swag.) Beginning 11" from 1 short edge (top), **fuse** web tape along each side edge on right side of each fabric piece (**Fig. 1**). Do not remove paper backing.

Fig. 1

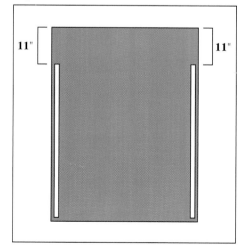

4. **Fuse** web tape along bottom edge on wrong side of each fabric piece. Do not remove paper backing.

5. Remove paper backing from side edges only. Matching right sides, place fabric pieces together as shown in **Fig. 2**. **Fuse** side edges of fabric pieces together. Turn right side out and press along side edges. Remove paper from remaining tape and **fuse** edges in place. Use 11" lengths of web tape to **fuse** each side edge of each fabric piece to wrong side at each end of swag (**Fig. 3**).

Fig. 2

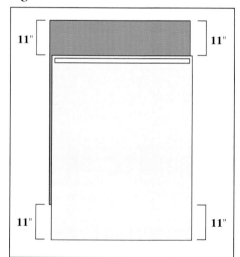

Fig. 3

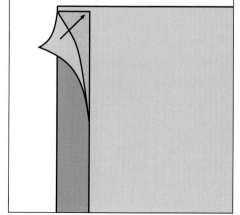

DRAPERIES WITH SWAG VALANCE (Continued)

6. For casing at each end of swag, make a 1" **single hem** along edge. **Fuse** web tape along hemmed edge on wrong side. Do not remove paper backing. Press edge 5½" to wrong side, overlapping edge over contrasting fabric. Unfold edge and remove paper backing. Refold edge and **fuse** in place.

7. Remove rod from window and insert through 1 casing of each swag; twist each swag and insert rod through remaining casing of each swag. Adjust gathers evenly across rod. Hang valance.

DIAGRAM

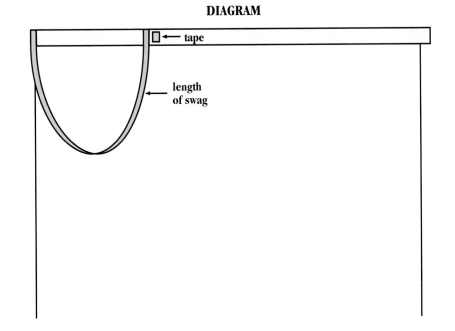

tape

length of swag

POUF TABLE SKIRT WITH FRINGED TABLE TOPPER

(Shown on page 7)

For table skirt, you will need a round table, fabric, and 1"w paper-backed fusible web tape.

For table topper, you will need fabric, 1"w paper-backed fusible web tape, 6"w cotton bullion fringe, fabric glue, and spring-type clothespins.

TABLE SKIRT

1. Measure table for floor length skirt. Add 40" to the determined measurement. Cut a square of fabric the determined measurement, **piecing fabric panels** as necessary.

2. Make a 1" **single hem** along all edges of fabric square.

3. Center skirt on table. Tuck hemmed edge of fabric under at floor and arrange folds for "pouf" effect.

TABLE TOPPER

1. Measure table to determine desired length of side edges of table topper; add 2". Cut a fabric square the determined measurement.

2. Make a 1" **single hem** along all edges of fabric square. With fringe extending beyond edge of fabric square, glue bound edge of fringe along edge on wrong side of fabric square; secure fringe with clothespins until glue is dry.

> The projects on these pages require the use of the following techniques which are shown in **bold print** in the instructions. Please familiarize yourself with the General Instructions, pages 118 - 127, and these specific techniques before beginning the projects.
>
> - *Measuring Tables (page 120)*
> - *Fusing (page 123)*
> - *Piecing Fabric Panels (page 123)*
> - *Making a Single Hem (page 124)*
> - *Making a Double Hem (page 124)*

You will need a decorative pole curtain rod, fabric (we used a 10 yd length of 48"w sheer fabric for our 48"w x 60"h window), 1/2"w paper-backed fusible web tape, 2 styles of decorative cord, 2 tassels, a cup hook, hot glue gun, and glue sticks.

1. Mount curtain rod.

2. (**Note:** Refer to **Diagram** for Step 2.) To determine length of fabric panel, drape a tape measure over rod to determine placement and length of each swag and cascade (tape measure should be draped along desired lower edge of each swag). Make a note of the measurement for each swag and cascade; add measurements together (to achieve a "puddle" effect at the floor, we added approx. 3 yds to the rod-to-floor measurement for the long cascade). Cut 1 length of fabric and 1 length of each style of cord the determined measurement.

*The projects on these pages require the use of the following techniques which are shown in **bold print** in the instructions. Please familiarize yourself with the General Instructions, pages 118 - 127, and these specific techniques before beginning the projects.*

- *Fusing (page 123)*
- *Making a Single Hem (page 124)*
- *Painted Box with Padded Lid (page 19)*

3. Make a 1/2" **single hem** along each end of fabric length. If desired, make a 1/2" **single hem** along each long edge of fabric length.

4. Drape fabric on rod, using measurements obtained in Step 2 to achieve the desired effect. If "puddle" effect is desired, tuck end of fabric under at floor and arrange folds. It may be helpful to use a rubber band to gather end of fabric before tucking it under.

5. Glue 1 tassel to 1 end of each cord length. Using draped fabric as a guide, drape each cord separately over fabric. Use cup hook to secure cords to wall.

DIAGRAM

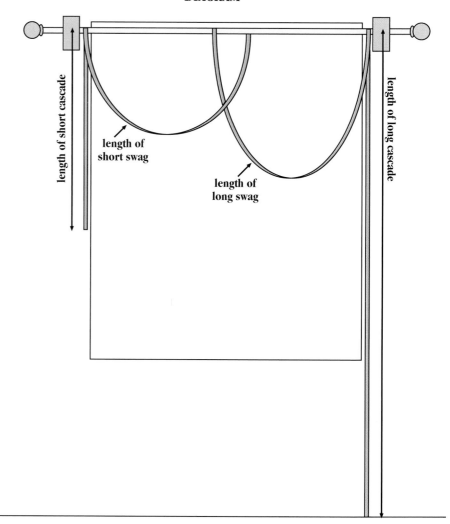

FABRIC-COVERED PICTURE FRAMES (Shown on page 7)

For each frame, you will need a purchased precut mat for frame front (we used a 6" x 7" mat with a 3" x 4" opening and an 8" x 10" mat with a 4½" x 6½" opening), a piece of mat board same size as precut mat for frame back, a piece of mat board for frame stand (a 2" x 5" piece for small frame; a 2" x 7" piece for large frame), fabric, removable fabric marking pen, spring-type clothespins, spray adhesive, hot glue gun, glue sticks, fabric glue, 3/16" dia. twisted cording with ½" lip to trim outer edge of frame, and other desired trims (we used ⅛" dia. twisted cord, ⅝"w and ⅞"w fringe, ⅜"w trim, ½"w gimp trim, ⅝"w and ¾"w loop fringe, and 8mm and 15mm pearl half-beads).

1. To cover frame front, use fabric marking pen to draw around mat and mat opening on wrong side of fabric. Cutting 1" from drawn lines, cut out shape; at corners of opening in fabric, clip fabric to ⅛" from drawn lines (**Fig. 1**).

Fig. 1

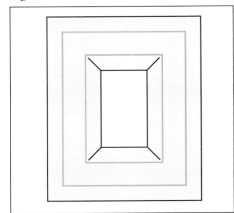

2. Apply spray adhesive to front of mat. Center mat, adhesive side down, on fabric and press in place. Fold fabric edges at opening of mat to back over edges of mat and hot glue in place. Fold corners of fabric diagonally over corners of mat and hot glue

in place (**Fig. 2**). Fold remaining fabric edges to back of mat and hot glue in place.

Fig. 2

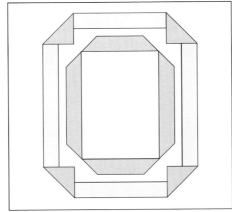

3. (**Note:** Use fabric glue for Steps 3 - 5. When gluing, secure trims with clothespins until glue is dry. To prevent ends of cording from fraying after cutting, apply fabric glue to ½" of cording around area to be cut, allow to dry, and then cut.) To trim frame front, begin at bottom edge of frame front and glue lip of 3/16" dia. cording along outer edge on wrong side of frame front. Glue desired trim(s) along inner edge of frame front.

4. For each flower, cut an approx. 3" length of loop fringe. Overlap ends of loop fringe and form fringe into a circle with straight edge gathered at center (see **Fig. 1** of **Painted Box with Padded Lid**); glue in place. Glue a pearl half-bead to center of flower. Glue flower to frame.

5. For cord with tassels, cut cord desired length. With fringe extending beyond end of cord, wrap and glue a length of fringe around each end of cord; glue a length of trim around top of fringe. Glue cord to frame front.

6. To cover frame back, measure width of mat board for frame back; add 2". Measure height of mat board; double measurement and add 2". Cut a piece of fabric the determined measurements.

7. Apply spray adhesive to 1 side of mat board. Place mat board, adhesive side down, on fabric piece and press in place (**Fig. 3**). Fold side edges of fabric to wrong side along side edges of mat board and hot glue in place. Fold bottom edge of fabric over mat board and hot glue in place. Fold top edge of fabric 1" to wrong side and hot glue in place. For back of frame back, fold top half of fabric over mat board and hot glue along edges to secure.

Fig. 3

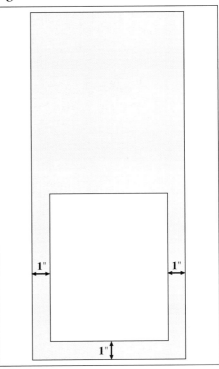

8. With right side of frame back facing wrong side of frame front, hot glue side and bottom edges of frame back to frame front, leaving opening at top for inserting photo.

9. To cover frame stand, repeat Steps 6 and 7. Fold top edge of frame stand 1½" to right side. With frame stand centered right side up on back of frame and bottom of frame stand even with bottom of frame, hot glue area of frame stand above fold to back of frame.

COUNTRY WEST

*R*ugged yet inviting, a cowboy-inspired decor offers an interesting mix of Old West, Native American, and Mexican influences. In this decidedly Western atmosphere, a blend of bold and subtle hues reflects the mood of the Painted Desert. Streaked across a stunning bedspread, dramatic shades of crimson and emerald yield to mellow tones of terra-cotta and parchment. Rib-textured pillowcases in coordinating colors summon the weary cowpoke to kick off his boots and rest a spell. As handsome as the dappled ponies it represents, the floorcloth is easy to make using fabric cutouts. Extending the theme throughout your home, the two window treatments in this section let you go country casual in no time. Simple accessories like our decorated planters and fabric-covered picture frames are fun and extra-easy to make. This collection will have you branded a decorating whiz before sunset!

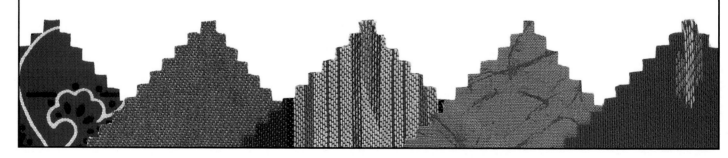

Bunkhouse Bedspread, page 33
Pillowcases, page 33

25

*Y*ou don't have to ride out on the range to enjoy the feisty spirit of pinto ponies. This simple floorcloth (right) brings their playful appeal right into your home. Created with fabric spots that are fused to artist's canvas, the rug has an alternating prairie point edging of rust and black checks and red bandannas. Even easier to make, our decorated planters (below) are outfitted in classic cowboy style — chambray, conchas, rope, and a bandanna.

A focal point for this Western decor is the casual swag and cascade window treatment (opposite). A length of tawny burlap is simply draped over a wooden stick and puddled on the floor. Mounted on one side of the rod, a pair of antlers stimulates visual interest.

Pinto Floorcloth, page 34
Western Planters, page 31

Casual Swag and Cascade, page 35

27

*S*cattered about your home, family photos are reflections of your unique style. Bits of Western memorabilia make these fabric-covered picture frames (right) a novel way to display your treasured keepsakes. The cowboy lamp is a lighthearted piece, with its shade wearing a blue jean pocket and its base stuffed with chili peppers and rope. Floor pillows (below) in harmonizing prints continue the theme. Leather lacing threaded through punched holes gives the chambray envelope pillow its rustic appearance. The others are easily created with corner ties.

Expand the mood with a simple tab window shade (opposite). The reversible chambray and bandanna print curtain has eye-catching hanging loops made from conchas and leather strips.

Tab Window Shade, page 34

CORNER-TIED FLOOR PILLOWS

(Shown on page 28)

For each pillow, you will need two 25" fabric squares, one 18" square pillow form, 1"w paper-backed fusible web tape, four 12" lengths of 1/8"w leather lacing, and 4 conchas (for concha pillow only).

1. Make a 1" **single hem** along each edge of each fabric square.

2. Center pillow form on wrong side of 1 fabric square. Center remaining fabric square right side up on pillow form.

3. For pillow tied with lacing only, overlap edges of fabric squares and gather fabric together at 1 corner of pillow form. Wrap 1 lacing length around gathered area and tie ends to secure. Repeat for remaining corners.

4. For concha pillow, overlap edges of fabric squares and gather fabric together at 1 corner of pillow form. Wrap 1 lacing length around gathered area, thread lacing ends through concha, and tie ends into a bow. Repeat for remaining corners.

ENVELOPE FLOOR PILLOW (Shown on page 28)

You will need one 22" x 17" fabric piece for pillow front and one 22" x 30" fabric piece for pillow back, 50" of 1/8"w leather lacing, 1"w paper-backed fusible web tape, fabric marking pen, liquid fray preventative, 1/8" hole punch, polyester fiberfill, hot glue gun, and glue sticks.

1. Make a 1" **single hem** along 1 long edge (top) of pillow front fabric piece.

2. Fuse web tape on right side of pillow front along side and bottom edges. Remove paper backing.

3. Referring to **Fig. 1**, match right sides and **fuse** bottom and side edges of pillow front and pillow back together. Do not clip seam allowances at corners. Turn pillow right side out and carefully push corners outward, making sure seam allowances lie flat; press.

Fig. 1

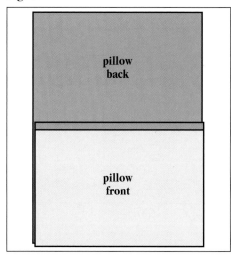

4. For flap, make a 1" **single hem** along top and side edges of pillow back (**Fig. 2**). Refer to **Fig. 3** and **fuse** a 6" length of web tape along each side edge on wrong side of pillow flap. Do not remove paper backing. Press top edge of flap 6" to wrong side. Unfold edge and remove paper backing. Refold edge and **fuse** in place.

Fig. 2

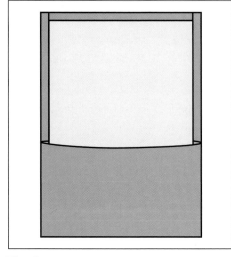

Fig. 3

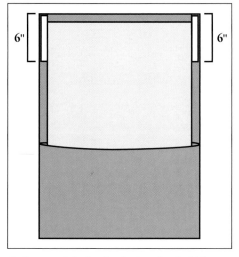

5. To punch holes for lacing, begin 3/4" from 1 side edge of flap and use fabric marking pen to mark dots 1" apart 1" from top edge of flap. Apply a small amount of fray preventative at each dot; allow to dry. Punch a hole through fabric at each dot using hole punch.

6. Beginning and ending on wrong side of flap, lace lacing through holes; trim ends if necessary and glue ends to secure.

7. Stuff pillow with fiberfill. Fold flap over front of pillow; glue edges of flap in place.

WESTERN PLANTERS (Shown on page 26)

Any plant will take on Western flair when planted in these flowerpots. We "planted" artificial cacti in our 4¹/₂", 5³/₄", and 7³/₄" high pots and covered the floral foam with dried beans. To give larger plants more stability, we covered the holes in the bottom of the pots and weighted the pots with aquarium gravel before filling them with floral foam.

BANDANNA-TRIMMED PLANTER

You will need desired size clay pot, a bandanna, hot glue gun, and glue sticks.

1. Fold bandanna in half diagonally. Wrap bandanna around rim of pot and knot ends together; tuck point of bandanna under fabric at rim.
2. Glue bandanna to pot.

CONCHA-TRIMMED PLANTER

You will need desired size clay pot, ¹/₄" dia. rope, large conchas, hot glue gun, and glue sticks.

1. Measure around rim of pot; add 18". Cut a length of rope the determined measurement.
2. Beginning and ending approx. 9" from ends of rope and spacing conchas evenly, thread conchas onto rope.
3. Wrap rope around rim of pot. Knot ends of rope together. Glue conchas to pot to secure. Trim ends of rope.

ROPE-TRIMMED PLANTER

You will need desired size clay pot, ¹/₄" dia. rope, fabric, hot glue gun, and glue sticks.

1. Measure around rim of pot; add 1". Measure width of rim of pot. Cut a strip of fabric the determined measurements.
2. Press each long edge of fabric strip ¹/₄" to wrong side; press 1 short edge of fabric strip ¹/₄" to wrong side.

3. Beginning with unpressed end, glue fabric strip around center of pot rim.
4. Measure around rim of pot; add 16". Cut 2 lengths of rope the determined measurement.
5. Place rope lengths side by side and glue lengths together at center. Matching glued area of lengths to overlapped area of fabric trim, glue lengths halfway around rim along center of fabric trim.
6. Glue remainder of lengths to pot as shown in **Fig. 1**.

Fig. 1

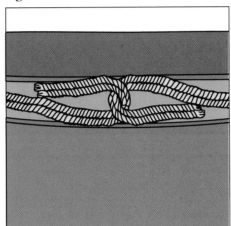

COUNTRY WEST LAMP
(Shown on page 28)

You will need desired size canning jar for lamp base, jar lid lamp kit, lampshade, fabric to cover lampshade, ¹/₄" dia. rope, 1 back pocket cut from a pair of blue jeans, 1 bandanna, wood excelsior, artificial chili peppers, tissue paper, fabric glue, spray adhesive, hot glue gun, glue sticks, and removable tape.

1. Cover lampshade with fabric.
2. For trim along top edge of shade, measure around top of shade. Cut a length of rope the determined measurement. Beginning at shade seamline, hot glue rope along top edge of shade. Repeat for bottom edge of shade.
3. Hot glue side and bottom edges of pocket to front of shade. Cut bandanna into quarters. Folding pieces as desired, insert 2 bandanna quarters into pocket. Discard remaining bandanna quarters.
4. For lamp base, cut a length of rope. Place 1 end of rope in bottom of jar. Twisting rope loosely as the jar is filled, arrange rope, excelsior, and peppers in jar.
5. Follow lamp kit manufacturer's instructions to assemble lamp. Place shade on lamp.

HORSESHOE FRAME (Shown on page 28)

For frame to fit a 3" x 5" photograph, you will need heavy (corrugated) cardboard, one 8" x 10" fabric piece to cover frame, low-loft polyester bonded batting, 1/4" dia. rope, 4" of 5/8"w grosgrain ribbon, 1 horseshoe, fabric marking pen, craft knife, tracing paper, hot glue gun, and glue sticks.

1. For frame front, frame back, and stand, use craft knife to cut one 6" x 8" piece, one 5 3/4" x 7 3/4" piece, and one 2" x 5 1/2" piece from cardboard.

2. For frame front, trace oval pattern onto tracing paper; cut out. Draw around pattern on center of 6" x 8" cardboard piece; use craft knife to cut out opening.

3. To pad frame front, place frame front on batting. Use fabric marking pen to draw around frame front edge and frame front opening on batting; cut out batting. Glue batting to frame front.

4. Center frame front on wrong side of fabric piece and use fabric marking pen to draw around opening; remove frame front. Referring to **Fig. 1**, cut fabric piece from center top to center bottom of oval to 1/8" from drawn line; at 1/2" intervals, clip fabric to 1/8" from drawn line.

Fig. 1

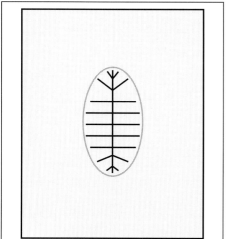

5. Center frame front, batting side down, on wrong side of fabric piece. Alternating sides, fold clipped fabric edges over edge of opening to back of frame front; glue in place. Fold fabric corners diagonally over corners of frame front; glue in place (**Fig. 2**). Fold remaining fabric edges over edges to back of frame front, pulling fabric until smooth; glue in place.

Fig. 2

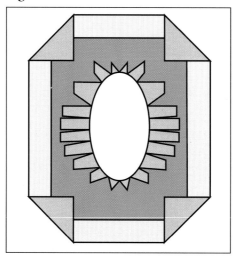

6. Glue a length of rope around edge of frame front, trimming ends to fit. Repeat for frame opening. Glue horseshoe to frame front.

7. For frame back, center 5 3/4" x 7 3/4" cardboard piece on back of frame front. Glue side and bottom edges of frame back in place.

8. For stand, fold 1 end (top) of 2" x 5 1/2" cardboard piece 1 1/2" to 1 side (right side). With bottom of stand extending 1/2" below frame bottom, glue wrong side of top of stand to center of frame back (**Fig. 3**). Glue 1 end of ribbon 1/2" above center bottom of frame back; glue remaining end of ribbon to back of frame stand.

Fig. 3

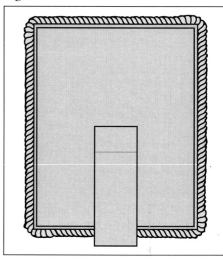

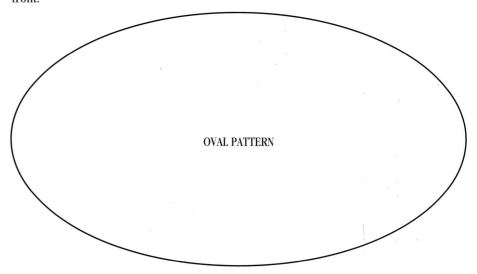

OVAL PATTERN

CONCHA FRAME (Shown on page 28)

For frame to fit a 5" x 7" photograph, you will need 1 purchased precut 8" x 10" mat with a 4¹/₂" x 6¹/₂" opening for frame front, one 7³/₄" x 9³/₄" piece of mat board for frame back, one 10" x 12" fabric piece to cover frame, leather for frame trim, four 1¹/₂"w conchas, fabric marking pen, sawtooth hanger, craft knife, hot glue gun, and glue sticks.

1. To cover frame front, center mat on wrong side of fabric piece and use fabric marking pen to draw around mat opening; remove mat. Cutting 1" from drawn lines, cut out opening; at corners of opening, clip fabric to ¹/₈" from drawn lines (**Fig. 1**).

Fig. 1

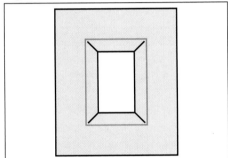

2. Center mat on wrong side of fabric piece. Fold fabric edges at opening of mat over edges to back of mat; glue in place. Fold fabric corners diagonally over corners of mat; glue in place (**Fig. 2**). Fold remaining fabric edges over edges to back of mat; glue in place.

Fig. 2

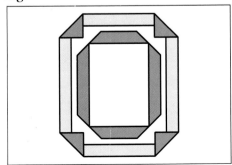

3. Use craft knife to cut two ¹/₄" x 8" and two ¹/₄" x 10" strips of leather; trim ends diagonally. Thread 1 concha onto center of each leather strip; glue strips to frame front.
4. Center frame back on back of frame front. Glue side and bottom edges of frame back in place. Glue sawtooth hanger 1" from top center on frame back.

PILLOWCASES (Shown on page 25)

For each pillowcase, you will need a bed pillow, fabric, ³/₄"w paper-backed fusible web tape, and fabric marking pen.

1. Referring to **Fig. 1**, measure length of pillow; measure around width of pillow. Add 12" to length measurement and 2" to width measurement. Cut fabric the determined measurements. Use fabric marking pen to mark edges that equal the determined length measurement.

Fig. 1

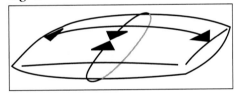

2. Fuse web tape on right side of fabric along both marked edges and 1 unmarked edge. Remove paper backing.
3. Matching right sides and marked edges, fold fabric in half; **fuse** edges together. Press seam allowance on marked edge to 1 side.
4. Make a 3¹/₂" **double hem** along remaining raw edge of fabric.
5. Do not clip seam allowances at corners. Turn pillowcase right side out and carefully push corners outward, making sure seam allowances lie flat; press.

---

*The projects on these pages require the use of the following techniques which are shown in **bold print** in the instructions. Please familiarize yourself with the General Instructions, pages 118 - 127, and these specific techniques before beginning the projects.*

- *Measuring Beds (page 120)*
- *Fusing (page 123)*
- *Piecing Fabric Strips (page 123)*
- *Piecing Fabric Panels (page 123)*
- *Making a Double Hem (page 124)*
- *Making Binding (page 125)*

BUNKHOUSE BEDSPREAD
(Shown on page 25)

You will need fabric for bedspread, fabric for binding, and ⁵/₈"w paper-backed fusible web tape.

1. Measure bed to determine finished size of bedspread. Cut bedspread fabric the determined measurements, **piecing fabric panels** as necessary.
2. Measure 1 short edge of bedspread fabric. Cut two 2⁵/₈"w strips of binding fabric the determined measurement, **piecing fabric strips** as necessary. **Make binding** from fabric strips.
3. Insert 1 short edge of bedspread fabric into fold of 1 binding length; **fuse** in place. Repeat for remaining short edge of bedspread fabric.
4. Measure 1 long edge of bedspread fabric; add 1". Cut two 2⁵/₈"w strips of binding fabric the determined measurement, **piecing fabric strips** as necessary. Press ends of strips ¹/₂" to wrong side. **Make binding** from fabric strips.
5. Repeat Step 3 to apply binding to long edges of bedspread fabric.

PINTO FLOORCLOTH (Shown on page 26)

For a 43" x 77½" floorcloth, you will need a 49" x 76" piece of unprimed artist's canvas, brown fabric for pinto spots, 2 coordinating fabrics for prairie point edging, paper-backed fusible web, two 45" lengths of extra-wide double-fold bias tape, clear polyurethane sealer, large foam brush, rolling pin, masking tape, and craft glue.

1. For pinto spots, **fuse** web to wrong side of brown fabric. Cut desired size spots from fabric. Remove paper backing. **Fuse** spots to 1 side (right side) of canvas.
2. (**Note:** Keep canvas flat at all times.) Tape canvas, right side up, to a covered work surface. Apply 1 coat of sealer to right side of canvas. Allow to dry (canvas will shrink slightly and curl at edges). Remove tape.
3. Use a pressing cloth and a warm dry iron to press canvas flat. Allow to cool. Trimming off any edges that do not lie flat, cut canvas to 45" x 72".
4. To finish edges of canvas, draw a diagonal line on wrong side of canvas across each corner as shown in **Fig. 1**. Cut off corners along drawn lines. Fold edges of canvas 1" to wrong side; glue to secure. Use rolling pin to flatten folded edges.

Fig. 1

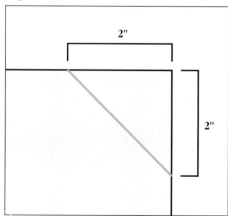

5. Allowing to dry between coats, apply 2 coats of sealer to right side of floorcloth.
6. For prairie point edging, cut seven 9½" squares from each coordinating fabric.
7. For each prairie point, press 1 fabric square in half diagonally with wrong sides together; press in half again, forming a triangle (**Fig. 2**).

Fig. 2

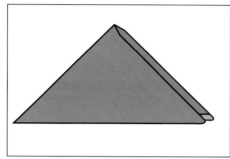

8. Referring to **Fig. 3** and alternating fabrics, insert raw edges of 7 prairie points into fold of 1 bias tape length, spacing prairie points evenly. Glue in place. Repeat for remaining bias tape length and prairie points.

Fig. 3

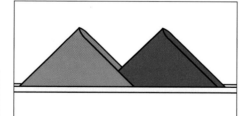

9. Place 1 bias tape length on wrong side of floorcloth along 1 short edge (side) with tops of prairie points extending approx. 3¾" beyond side edge of floorcloth. Fold ends of bias tape length to wrong side as necessary to make prairie points even with top and bottom edges of floorcloth; glue ends in place. Glue entire length of bias tape to floorcloth. Repeat for remaining length of bias tape.

TAB WINDOW SHADE
(Shown on page 29)

You will need 2 coordinating fabrics for shade, leather for tabs, 1"w paper-backed fusible web tape, 2¼"w conchas, 1" dia. wooden dowel, mounting brackets to fit dowel, paint to match window trim, paintbrush, saw, safety pin, hot glue gun, and glue sticks.

1. **Measure window** to obtain "inside" measurements; add 2" to width measurement. Cut 1 piece from each fabric the determined measurements.
2. For shade, omit Step 4 and follow **Making a Pillow**.
3. To determine number of conchas needed, divide inside window width measurement by 3, rounding up to the next whole number.
4. For tabs, cut one ½" x 9½" strip from leather for each concha; trim 1 end to a point. Thread 1 tab through each concha, with pointed end extending 2" beyond 1 end of concha; glue concha to tab.
5. Spacing conchas evenly, glue conchas to front of shade along top edge as shown in **Fig. 1**.

Fig. 1

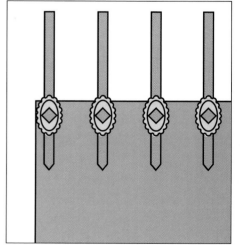

TAB WINDOW SHADE (continued)

6. Glue 1¼" of remaining end of each tab to back of shade, forming loops.

7. Mount brackets in window. Cut dowel ½" shorter than inside width of window. Paint brackets and dowel.

8. Insert dowel through loops on shade; hang shade.

9. Fold 1 corner of shade to right side; use safety pin to secure. Remove shade from window. Press fold. Hang shade again.

*The projects on these pages require the use of the following techniques which are shown in **bold print** in the instructions. Please familiarize yourself with the General Instructions, pages 118 - 127, and these specific techniques before beginning the projects.*

- *Measuring Windows (page 120)*
- *Fusing (page 123)*
- *Making a Pillow (page 127)*

CASUAL SWAG AND CASCADE (Shown on page 27)

You will need an approx. 2" dia. wooden stick several inches longer than width of window for rod, brackets for mounting stick (we substituted mounted deer antlers for 1 bracket), and 48"w burlap fabric (we used approx. 7½ yds for our 36"w x 72"h window).

1. Mount brackets at window. Place stick in brackets.

2. (**Note:** Refer to **Diagram** for Step 2.) To determine length of fabric needed, measure from top of mounted stick to floor for cascade at 1 side of window; add 10" for "puddling." Measure from top of rod to desired finished length for cascade at remaining side of window. Use 1 or more tape measures to determine lengths of swag(s). Add all measurements together. Add 6" to total measurement. Cut fabric the determined length.

3. Fringe 3" at each end of fabric length.

4. Drape fabric over stick, using measurements determined in Step 2 to achieve the desired effect.

DIAGRAM

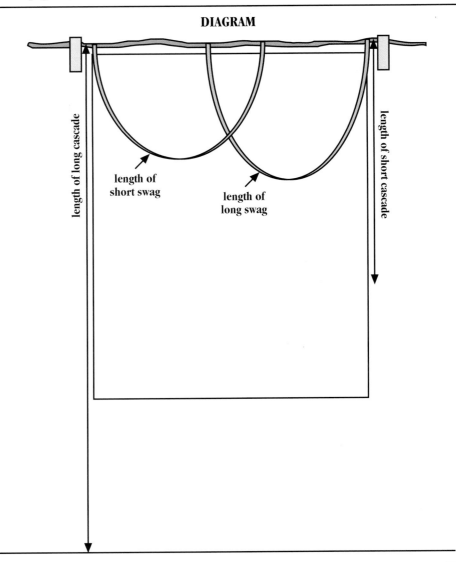

length of long cascade

length of short cascade

length of short swag

length of long swag

Romancing The Past

Dressed in elegant textures and tenderly blushed colors, the Victorian home was the epitome of refinement and beauty. Each room was a showcase of rich fabrics, polished wood, and lacy touches; however, it was a love for the natural beauty of flowers that most typified the turn-of-the-century home. At every opportunity, fresh cuttings from the garden perfumed the air with their heady scent. This genteel lifestyle is celebrated in our lace-trimmed collection for a lady's boudoir (or any room that calls for a bit of femininity). Embellished with a variety of pretty fabrics including floral prints and stripes in soft shades of pink, green, and ivory, even the most humble furnishings and accents become reflections of this romantic era. Our German statice wreath blooms with silk roses and hydrangea and plump ''flowers'' made from handkerchiefs and silk berries. Swirls of decorative ribbons add a finishing touch. Airy lace panels provide graceful — and very simple — backdrops for this section's two window treatments, which feature a handkerchief valance and a flower bonnet accent. Filled with such beautiful lace and flowers, your home will be graced with the romance of the past.

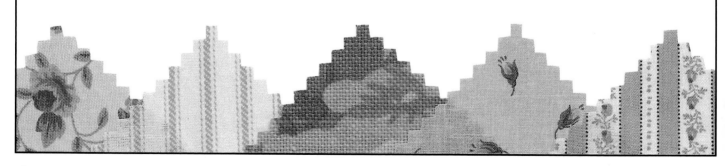

Wreath with Handkerchief ''Flowers,'' page 46

Battenberg Lace Lampshade, page 47
Pouf Table Skirt with Lace Table Topper, page 43

*T*he Victorians enjoyed furnishing their homes to provide a soothing respite from the cares of the day. A table skirt (opposite) in a large floral print is tucked under at the floor, and its folds are arranged to create a poufed effect. A simple square of creamy lace tops the skirt, creating lovely points all around. Tiny sprays of silk and paper flowers adorn the topper and are echoed on the lampshade cover. An illuminating piece for this romantic scene, the cover is made by threading ribbon through Battenberg lace table runners and gathering them around a purchased lampshade. Covered with a petite rosebud fabric, a cardboard chest of drawers (below, left) becomes a feminine lingerie chest. Lace doilies encircling the decorative drawer pulls add to its beauty. Held in place with wired silk ribbon bows, a lace table runner dresses up a chair (below, right).

Lingerie Chest, page 44
Lacy Chair Decoration, page 43

A visual delight, the delicate lace window shade (right) is a breeze to create from a single fabric panel. Decorated with ribbon-tied nosegays, the handkerchief valance is attached with fusible web tape. Accent pillows for the bed (below) are fashioned in subtle Victorian hues and trimmed with ribbons, lace, and a nosegay. The roll pillow has a lacy fused-on heart, the square pillow is made from a table runner, and the round pillow is gathered with a rubber band.

A flower-trimmed hat provides a refreshing focal point for the bishop's sleeve curtains (opposite). Pretty in pink and white, the panels are poufed with tissue paper!

Lace Window Shade with Handkerchief Valance, page 47
Roll Pillow, page 42
Lacy Envelope Pillow, page 42
Round Pillow, page 47

Bishop's Sleeve Curtains with Lace Sheer, page 46

ROLL PILLOW

(Shown on page 40)

You will need a 22" x 35" fabric piece for pillow; one 10¼" x 22" fabric strip, two 2½" x 22" bias fabric strips, two 22" lengths of 1¼"w lace, and a 4½"w heart-shaped Battenberg lace doily for trim; two 30" lengths of 1"w satin ribbon; 2 strong rubber bands; polyester fiberfill; paper-backed fusible web; aluminum foil; and ¾"w paper-backed fusible web tape.

1. For wide fabric trim, make a ¾" **single hem** along each long edge of 10¼" x 22" fabric strip. **Fuse** web tape along each hemmed edge on wrong side of fabric strip. Remove paper backing and place fabric strip wrong side up.

2. For bias trim along each long edge of wide fabric trim, **fuse** web tape along 1 long edge on wrong side of each 2½" x 22" bias strip. Do not remove paper backing. With wrong sides together, press strip in half lengthwise. Unfold strip and remove paper backing. Refold strip and **fuse** long edges together.

3. With raw edge of 1 bias trim strip overlapping web along 1 long edge of wide fabric trim, **fuse** bias strip along wide trim. Repeat to **fuse** remaining bias strip along remaining long edge of wide trim.

4. Place a large piece of aluminum foil, shiny side up, on ironing board. Place lace lengths and doily, wrong side up, on foil. Cover lace and doily with a piece of web. **Fuse** web to lace and doily; allow to cool. Remove paper backing. Peel lace and doily from foil. Trim excess web from lace and doily edges. **Fuse** 1 length of lace ¾" from each side edge of fabric trim. **Fuse** doily to center of fabric trim.

5. **Fuse** web to wrong side of fabric trim. Remove paper backing. Matching short edges of trim to long edges of pillow fabric piece, **fuse** fabric trim along center on right side of pillow fabric piece.

6. On right side of pillow fabric piece, **fuse** web tape along long edges. On wrong side of pillow fabric piece, **fuse** web tape along short edges. Remove paper backing from long edges only. Matching right sides, fold fabric piece in half lengthwise. **Fuse** long edges together to form a tube; press seam allowance to 1 side. Press remaining raw edges 5" to wrong side. Unfold edges and remove paper backing. Refold edges and **fuse** in place. Turn tube right side out.

7. Wrap 1 rubber band around 1 end of tube 3" from end. Stuff tube with fiberfill and wrap remaining rubber band around tube 3" from remaining end.

8. Tie 1 ribbon length into a bow around each end of pillow, covering rubber bands; trim ribbon ends.

LACY ENVELOPE PILLOW

(Shown on page 40)

You will need a 34½" length cut from 1 end of a lace-trimmed table runner (we used a 16½"w runner), lightweight fabric to match runner and paper-backed fusible web for lining (optional), ¾"w paper-backed fusible web tape, polyester fiberfill, two 30" lengths of ribbon for bow (we used 1½"w decorative mesh ribbon and 1⅜"w wired silk ribbon), a 1" button, and fabric glue.

1. If lining is desired, cut a 23¾" length of fabric same width as fabric part of table runner piece. **Fuse** web to wrong side of fabric piece. Matching 1 short edge of fabric piece to cut edge (bottom edge) of runner piece, **fuse** fabric to center on wrong side of runner piece.

2. Make a ¾" **single hem** along cut edge (bottom edge) of table runner piece.

3. Referring to **Fig. 1**, **fuse** a 23" length of web tape along each side fabric edge on wrong side of runner piece; **fuse** web tape along top fabric edge on wrong side of runner piece. Do not remove paper backing.

Fig. 1

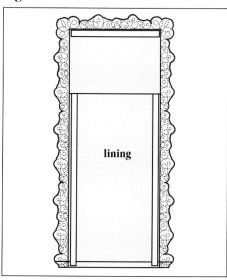

lining

4. For envelope, press bottom edge of runner piece 11½" to wrong side. For flap, press top edge of runner piece 10¾" to wrong side. Unfold. Remove paper backing from side edges of runner piece. Refold bottom edge and **fuse** side edges together.

5. Stuff pillow lightly with fiberfill. Remove paper backing from top edge. Fold flap over opening and **fuse** in place.

6. Tie ribbon lengths together into a bow; trim ends. Glue bow to pillow flap; glue button to bow.

POUF TABLE SKIRT WITH LACE TABLE TOPPER

(Shown on page 38)

For table skirt for round table, you will need fabric for skirt and 1"w paper-backed fusible web tape.

For table topper, you will need a purchased square lace table topper, fabric for liner, 1"w paper-backed fusible web tape, artificial flowers, florist wire, 1"w satin ribbon, wire cutters, and safety pins.

TABLE SKIRT

1. Measure table; add 40" to the determined measurement. Cut a fabric square the determined measurement, **piecing fabric panels** as necessary.

2. Make a 1" **single hem** along all edges of fabric square.

3. Center skirt on table. Tuck hemmed edge of fabric under at floor and arrange folds for "pouf" effect.

TABLE TOPPER

1. For liner, cut a square of fabric same size as lace table topper.

2. Make a 1" **single hem** along all edges of fabric square.

3. Center liner, then table topper, on table.

4. Use a safety pin on wrong side of topper and liner to gather topper and liner at center of each side edge (**Fig. 1**).

Fig. 1

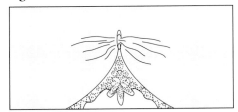

5. (**Note:** Follow Step 5 to make a total of 4 nosegays.) Wire flowers together. Form a double-loop bow from a length of ribbon; wrap bow with wire at center to secure. Wire bow to flowers. Pin nosegay over 1 gathered area on table topper.

LACY CHAIR DECORATION (Shown on page 39)

You will need a chair, a Battenberg lace-trimmed table runner (we used a 16$^1\!/_2$" x 36" runner for our 15$^1\!/_2$" long decoration), 1"w paper-backed fusible web tape, removable fabric marking pen, and two 1 yd lengths of 1$^1\!/_2$"w wired silk ribbon.

1. Measure from center top of chair back to desired length of decoration. On right side of table runner, use fabric marking pen and a ruler to mark a line the determined measurement from each end (**Fig. 1**).

Fig. 1

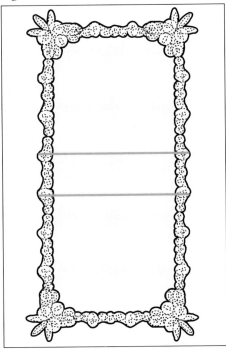

2. On right side of runner, **fuse** web tape along inside of each line (**Fig. 2**). Do not remove paper backing.

Fig. 2

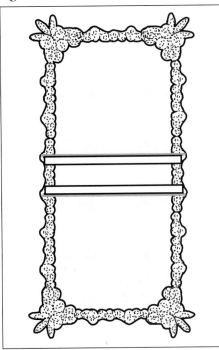

3. Matching right sides and short edges, press runner in half, making sure web tape lengths match. Unfold and remove paper backing. Refold and **fuse** runner together along web tape. With right sides out, press runner along fused area to form a crease at top of chair decoration.

4. Place decoration over chair back with crease at top and excess fabric at seam toward back of chair back. If desired, excess fabric may be trimmed close to seam.

5. To secure decoration on chair back, thread 1 length of ribbon through front and back of decoration at each side edge. Tie ribbons into bows; trim ends.

LINGERIE CHEST

(Shown on page 39)

You will need an unassembled cardboard 4-drawer chest (available at discount stores; our chest measures 26"h x 13"w x 12½"d assembled), fabric to cover chest (our chest required approx. 5 yds of 44/45"w fabric), paper-backed fusible web, ½"w paper-backed fusible web tape, four 4" dia. lace doilies, 4 decorative drawer pulls with screws to replace pulls that come with chest, washers to fit screws, craft knife, white poster board, fabric glue, hot glue gun, glue sticks, and matte white spray paint (optional; if see-through fabric is used).

1. If printed designs on chest pieces are visible through fabric, spray paint chest pieces before covering. Allow to dry.

2. (**Note:** Different manufacturers may refer to pieces of chest by different names; refer to figures for identification of pieces.) Lay chest piece on a flat surface. Measure length and width of center of chest piece (**Fig. 1**); add 4" to each measurement. Cut a piece of fabric the determined measurements.

Fig. 1

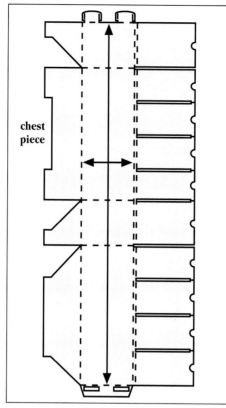

chest piece

3. Lay 1 shelf piece on a flat surface. Measure width of shelf piece at widest point (**Fig. 2**). Cut 1 fabric strip 3"w by the determined measurement for each shelf piece.

Fig. 2

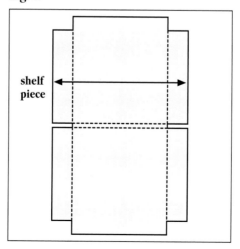

shelf piece

4. Lay 1 drawer piece on a flat surface. Measure length and width of drawer piece at widest points (**Fig. 3**); add 3" to each measurement. Cut 1 fabric piece the determined measurements for each drawer piece.

Fig. 3

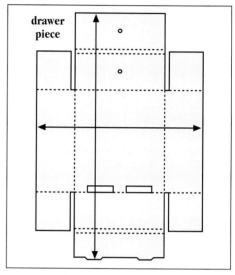

drawer piece

5. Fuse web to wrong sides of fabric pieces. Remove paper backing.

6. To cover chest piece, lay chest piece right side up on a flat surface. Center chest fabric piece, web side down, over measured area of chest piece. Beginning at center, **fuse** fabric piece to chest piece. Turn chest piece over. Trim excess fabric even with edges of chest piece; use craft knife to cut through fabric covering slits in chest piece.

7. To cover front edge of each shelf piece, lay 1 shelf piece right side up on a flat surface. Center fabric strip over center fold line on shelf piece (**Fig. 4**); **fuse** in place. Turn shelf piece over. Use craft knife to cut through fabric covering slits in shelf piece.

Fig. 4

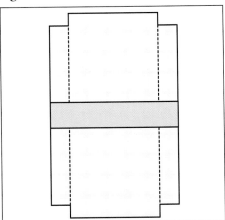

8. To cover each drawer piece, center 1 drawer piece wrong side up on wrong side of 1 drawer fabric piece. Alternating sides, fold edges of fabric over edges of drawer piece and **fuse** in place (**Fig. 5**). Turn drawer piece over. **Fuse** fabric piece to right side of drawer piece. Turn drawer piece over again. Trim excess fabric even with edges of drawer piece; use craft knife to cut through fabric covering slits and holes in drawer piece.

Fig. 5

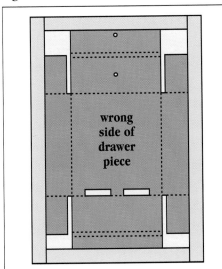

wrong side of drawer piece

9. To cover side edges of drawer fronts, measure height of 1 drawer front (**Fig. 6**). For each drawer, cut two 2⅝"w fabric strips the determined measurement. Make ⅝"w **binding** from each fabric strip.

Fig. 6

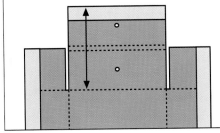

10. (**Note:** Follow Step 10 for each drawer.) With 1 end of 1 binding strip at bottom of 1 side edge of drawer front, insert side edge of drawer front into fold of binding strip and **fuse** in place; repeat for remaining side edge of drawer front (**Fig. 7**).

Fig. 7

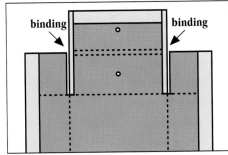

binding   binding

11. Omitting step for attaching drawer pulls to drawers, follow manufacturer's instructions to assemble chest.

12. For chest back, measure width and height of chest back; subtract ½" from each measurement. Cut poster board the determined measurements. Cut a piece of fabric 2" larger on all sides than poster board. **Fuse** web to wrong side of fabric piece. Center and **fuse** fabric piece to poster board. Fold corners of fabric diagonally to back of poster board; **fuse** in place. Fold remaining edges of fabric to back of poster board; **fuse** in place. Center and hot glue covered poster board to back of chest.

13. Use fabric glue to glue 1 doily over center of each drawer pull hole on each drawer front; allow to dry.

14. Using washers for spacers if needed, follow chest manufacturer's instructions to attach decorative drawer pulls to drawers.

WREATH WITH HANDKERCHIEF "FLOWERS"

(Shown on page 37)

You will need an 18" dia. white German statice wreath, dried and silk flowers (we used silk roses and dried and silk hydrangea), clusters of 1/2" dia. silk berries, handkerchiefs, rubber bands, 1"w silk wired ribbon, 1 1/2"w decorative mesh ribbon, florist wire, wire cutters, hot glue gun, and glue sticks.

1. For each handkerchief "flower," trim stems of 1 berry cluster to 2". Place stems of berry cluster at center of 1 handkerchief and wrap handkerchief around stems; secure with a rubber band (**Fig. 1**).

Fig. 1

2. Arrange dried flowers, silk flowers, and handkerchief "flowers" on wreath; glue to secure.
3. Form ribbons into a multi-loop bow; wrap bow with wire at center to secure. Glue bow and streamers to wreath.

BISHOP'S SLEEVE CURTAINS WITH LACE SHEER (Shown on page 41)

You will need 1 double curtain rod set or two 1/2" dia. spring-tension rods, fabric for curtains, lace fabric for sheer, 1"w and 1 1/2"w satin ribbon, 1"w paper-backed fusible web tape, string, cup hooks, tissue paper, straw hat, silk flowers, florist wire, wire cutters, hot glue gun, and glue sticks.

LACE SHEER

1. Mount curtain rods, allowing 2 1/2" for header on curtains.
2. To determine width of lace fabric panel for sheer, measure length of rod; multiply by 2 1/2. To determine length of lace fabric panel, measure from top of rod to desired length; add 11 1/4" for casing and hem. Cut 1 lace panel the determined measurements, **piecing fabric panels** as necessary.
3. Make a 1" **double hem** along each side edge of panel. Make a 4" **double hem** along bottom edge of panel.
4. For casing, make a 1" **single hem** along top edge of panel. **Fuse** web tape along top edge on wrong side of panel. Do not remove paper backing. Press edge 2 1/4" to wrong side. Unfold edge and remove paper backing. Refold edge and **fuse** in place.
5. Hang sheer.

CURTAINS

1. To determine width of each fabric panel for curtains, measure length of rod; multiply measurement by 1 1/4. To determine length of each panel, measure from top of rod to desired length; add 15" for header, casing, and hem and 12" for each pouf. Cut 2 fabric panels the determined measurements, **piecing fabric panels** as necessary.
2. For each panel, make a 1" **double hem** along each side edge of panel.

3. For header and casing on each panel, make a 1" **single hem** along top edge of panel. **Fuse** web tape along top edge on wrong side of panel. **Fuse** another length 2" below top edge. Do not remove paper backing. Press top edge of panel 4 1/2" to wrong side. Unfold edge and remove paper backing. Refold edge and **fuse** in place.
4. Hang curtains.
5. (**Note:** Work from top to bottom of each curtain panel to make each bishop's sleeve pouf.) For each pouf, attach a cup hook to window frame at desired position of bottom of pouf. Tie string around curtain panel approx. 6" below cup hook. Hang string over cup hook. Adjusting string along curtain panel as necessary, arrange pouf.
6. Use pins to mark desired finished length of curtains. Trim bottom edges of panels 8" below pins. Remove rod from window. Make a 4" **double hem** along bottom edge of each panel. Hang curtains again, stuffing poufs with tissue paper, if desired, to maintain shape.
7. Tie 1 length of each width of ribbon together into a bow around curtain below each pouf, covering string.
8. For hat, glue 1 1/2"w satin ribbon around crown. Arrange and glue silk flowers around back of crown. Form a double-loop bow from a length of 1 1/2"w ribbon; wrap bow with wire at center to secure. Tie a single-loop bow from a length of 1"w satin ribbon. Glue single-loop bow to center of double-loop bow. Glue bows to back of hat; trim ends.
9. To hang hat, fold an 18" length of string in half; glue fold of string to inside front of hat crown. Tie ends of string to rod between curtains.

LACE WINDOW SHADE WITH HANDKERCHIEF VALANCE (Shown on page 40)

You will need a curtain rod (we used a sash rod for a door window), lace fabric (we used lace tablecloth fabric), approx. 10" square handkerchiefs for valance, 2½"w lace trim, ½"w and 1½"w paper-backed fusible web tape, dried and silk flowers, florist wire, wire cutters, and 1 yd lengths of desired widths and colors of satin ribbon.

1. Mount curtain rod.

2. To determine width of lace fabric panel for shade, measure length of rod; add 2". To determine length of lace fabric panel, measure from top of rod to desired length; add 6¾". (**Note:** If bottom edge of lace fabric piece does not require a hem, add 5¾".) With center of lace pattern centered along length of panel, cut 1 piece from lace fabric the determined measurements.

3. Make a ½" **double hem** along each side edge of fabric piece. If necessary, make a ½" **double hem** along bottom edge of fabric piece. Make a ½" **single hem** along top edge of fabric piece.

4. For casing and header, **fuse** ½"w web tape along top edge on wrong side of shade. **Fuse** 1½"w web tape 1¾" below ½"w web tape. Do not remove paper backing. Press top edge of shade 3¾" to wrong side. Unfold edge and remove paper backing. Refold edge and **fuse** in place.

5. To determine number of handkerchiefs needed for valance, measure top edge of shade; add 2" and divide measurement by 7. Round number down to nearest whole number.

6. Press each handkerchief in half diagonally with right side out and decorative corner on 1 side; unfold. **Fuse** 1½"w web tape along each side of fold on wrong side of handkerchief. Remove paper backing and refold handkerchief.

7. At each end of top edge of shade, insert top edge of shade into fold of 1 handkerchief with decorative corner of handkerchief at front of shade and allowing handkerchiefs to extend approx. 1" beyond edge of shade; pin in place. Spacing remaining handkerchiefs evenly, insert top edge of shade into folds of remaining handkerchiefs; pin in place. **Fuse** handkerchiefs in place.

8. Cut a length of lace trim 1" longer than width of shade. Make a ½" **single hem** at each end of lace. **Fuse** 1½"w web tape along center on wrong side of lace. Center lace along top edge of shade with 1 long edge extending ¼" above top edge of shade; **fuse** in place.

9. For each nosegay at top of shade, wire flowers together; trim stems 1" below wire. Tie 4 ribbon lengths together into a bow; trim ends. Wire bow to flowers. With stems at top of shade, pin nosegay to shade.

10. Insert rod through casing and hang shade.

BATTENBERG LACE LAMPSHADE (Shown on page 38)

You will need a lampshade, 2 Battenberg lace table runners, ¼"w and 1"w satin ribbon, artificial flowers, florist wire, and wire cutters.

1. Measure height of lampshade; add 5". Measure around bottom edge of shade. Each table runner should measure approx. the determined measurements. For example, our 10" high shade that measures 38" around the bottom, required two 15" x 36" runners.

2. Measure around top edge of shade; add 24". Cut a length of ¼"w ribbon the determined measurement.

3. Place runners wrong side up and end to end. Beginning at 1 end of 1 runner, thread ¼"w ribbon through lace along top long edge of runner; continue to thread ribbon through lace along top edge of second runner. Pull ends of ribbon, gathering runners to fit top edge of shade. With right side out, wrap runners around shade and tie ribbon ends into a bow at front of shade.

4. For nosegay, wire flowers together. Make a double-loop bow from 1"w ribbon; wrap bow with wire at center to secure. Wire bow to flowers. Bend stems of flowers to form a "hook". Hook nosegay over top edge of shade.

ROUND PILLOW
(Shown on page 40)

You will need a 44" square of fabric, a 12" dia. pillow form, 1 strong rubber band, artificial flowers, florist wire, 1 yd of 1"w satin ribbon, wire cutters, a safety pin, and fabric glue.

1. Center pillow form on wrong side of fabric square.

2. Follow Steps 3 and 4 of **Pillow with Stenciled Bow**.

3. For nosegay, wire flowers together. Form a double-loop bow from ribbon; wrap bow with wire at center to secure. Wire bow to flowers. Use safety pin to pin nosegay to pillow next to "rosette."

French Country Charm

*B*ringing the exuberance of a warm country day indoors is as easy as creating this French Country collection for your kitchen or breakfast nook. Spring-fresh blues and white make the room sparkle, and brilliant bursts of sunflowers and yellow striped accents invite the sunshine inside. Each project is so simple to make that the entire ensemble can be completed in an evening or two! A few nips and tucks — secured with fusible web tape — let you create the place mats in minutes. Napkins fashioned from purchased dish towels are held with coordinating sunflower napkin ties, and a unique watering can centerpiece is easily sponge-painted and decorated with ribbon. This pristine scene is drawn together with a quick-and-easy window treatment — a single panel of French Toile fabric is hemmed with fusible web tape, hung with café curtain rings, and topped with a matching valance. Turn the page to discover more exciting accessories that you can create at home and add to your country collection!

Café Curtains with Lined Valance, page 60
Watering Can, page 61

49

Tea Cozy, page 56
Table Setting, page 58

*O*ur cheery setting is perfect for afternoon teatime. The blue checked teapot cozy (opposite) helps keep the brew steaming hot for refills. It's remarkably easy to complete using simple fusing methods. Fashioned from beribboned silk sunflowers, the napkin ties can be made in minutes!

A sunny dish towel and a silk sunflower are used to fashion a coordinating padded bar stool cover (left). Simply appliqué the sunflower design on the towel and tie the corners to the stool legs with bright grosgrain ribbons. "We're Glad You're Here" is the friendly message that emanates from the welcoming floorcloth (below). The mat is generously sprinkled with sunflowers and bordered with contrasting print fabrics in cheerful blue and white patterns.

Padded Bar Stool, page 55
"Welcome" Floorcloth, page 59

*O*rdinary *cotton dish towels (right) become lively fashion accents for your French Country kitchen. The jumbo fused-on sunflower on each one is actually made with a silk flower using a simple appliqué technique. Impressive as it looks cradling a batch of steaming hot rolls or muffins, the floral basket liner (bottom), bordered with navy blue grosgrain ribbon, is finished in no time using fabric glue. Lined with a coordinating blue checked fabric, a plain wooden tray becomes a special way to serve an afternoon repast.*

The sunflower clock will pace you through the best of times. A plain wooden battery-powered clock is magically transformed into a striking accent using paint, fabric, and a silk flower appliqué. As you can see, the hour and minute hands will keep you "right on the button."

Kitchen Clock, page 54

BASKET LINER

(Shown on page 52)

You will need a piece of fabric ³/₄" larger on all sides than desired finished size of liner, ¹/₄"w grosgrain ribbon, and fabric glue.

1. Press 1 edge of fabric piece ³/₈" to wrong side; press ³/₈" to wrong side again. Glue in place. Repeat for remaining edges.
2. For ribbon trim, cut 1 length of ribbon the same length as each edge of liner. Arrange ribbon lengths ¹/₂" from edges of liner; trim ribbon ends at a 45 degree angle to form mitered corners (**Fig. 1**). Glue ribbon lengths in place.

Fig. 1

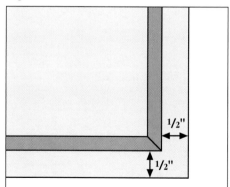

SILK FLOWER APPLIQUÉS

For each appliqué, you will need a silk flower (we used petal sections and leaves from 5"w sunflowers for projects in this section), fabric for flower center, paper-backed fusible web, and aluminum foil.

1. (**Note:** Follow all steps for each petal section to be made into an appliqué; omit Step 4 for each leaf.) Remove petal sections from stem, discarding any plastic or metal pieces.
2. Test for washability by washing 1 petal section. Do not use petal sections that are not colorfast.
3. Use a warm dry iron to press 1 petal section flat.

4. For flower center, **fuse** web to wrong side of fabric. Cut desired size circle from fabric. Remove paper backing. **Fuse** flower center to center of petal section.
5. Place a large piece of aluminum foil, shiny side up, on ironing board. Place flower, wrong side up, on foil. Cover flower with a square piece of web. **Fuse** web to wrong side of flower. Allow to cool. Remove paper backing. Peel flower from foil. Trim excess web from flower edges.
6. Follow project instructions to fuse flower appliqué to project.

KITCHEN CLOCK (Shown on page 53)

You will need an unfinished wooden clock (we used a 9¹/₂"w x 9"h x 2¹/₄"d clock from Walnut Hollow Farm®), battery-operated clock movement kit and clock hands, fine sandpaper, tack cloth, matte clear acrylic spray, white spray paint, poster board, fabric for clock face, 1 Silk Flower Appliqué (this page) to fit front of clock, silk leaves, 1"w grosgrain ribbon, embroidery floss, six ¹/₂" and eight ³/₈" buttons, paper-backed fusible web, craft knife, hot glue gun, and glue sticks.

1. Lightly sand clock until smooth; wipe with tack cloth to remove dust.
2. Allowing to dry between coats, spray clock with acrylic spray and then white paint.
3. For clock face, **fuse** web to wrong side of fabric. Remove paper backing. **Fuse** fabric to poster board. Cut fabric-covered poster board to fit front of clock.

4. **Fuse** silk flower appliqué to center of clock face.
5. Trace around hole at center of clock on poster board side of clock face; use craft knife to cut out hole.
6. Glue clock face to center front of clock.
7. Follow manufacturer's instructions to assemble and attach clock movement and hands to clock.
8. Thread floss through each button to resemble stitching. Glue floss ends to back of each button.
9. Glue one ¹/₂" button to clock face at 12, 3, 6, and 9 o'clock positions. Glue ³/₈" buttons to clock face at remaining hour positions.
10. Tie ribbon into a bow; trim ends. Glue bow knot and leaves to top of clock. Glue portions of streamers to top and side of clock. Glue remaining buttons to bow knot.

PADDED BAR STOOL
(Shown on page 51)

You will need a round bar stool, 1" thick foam rubber for pad, a woven cotton dish towel at least 6" wider than top of stool, 1 Silk Flower Appliqué (page 54), string, 3 yds of ³/8"w grosgrain ribbon, electric knife, fabric marking pen, and duct tape (optional).

1. Follow **Sunny Dish Towels**, this page, to fuse appliqué to center of towel.
2. Place stool, top side down, on foam rubber. Use fabric marking pen to draw around top of stool. Remove stool. Use electric knife to cut out foam rubber along drawn line.
3. Center foam rubber piece on stool. Center towel on stool as shown in **Fig. 1**.

Fig. 1

4. To secure towel, wrap a length of string around each towel corner and leg of stool; knot string and trim ends.
5. If desired, tape edges of towel to bottom of stool.
6. Cut ribbon into 4 equal lengths. Tie 1 length into a bow around each stool leg, covering string.

LINED SERVING TRAY (Shown on page 52)

You will need a wooden tray, fabric and 8-gauge clear vinyl (available at fabric stores) for tray lining, paper-backed fusible web, poster board, spray paint, hot glue gun, and glue sticks.

1. Spray paint tray; allow to dry.
2. Center tray on poster board and draw around bottom of tray. Cut out poster board along drawn lines. Place poster board piece in tray and trim to fit if necessary.
3. Fuse web to right side of fabric. Remove paper backing. Using a medium heat setting on iron and a pressing cloth (to keep vinyl from melting), **fuse** right side of fabric to vinyl.
4. Fuse web to wrong side of fabric. Do not remove paper backing.
5. Center poster board piece on paper backing side of fabric and draw around poster board. Cut out fabric 1" outside drawn line. Remove paper backing.
6. At ¹/2" intervals, make clips into edge of fabric to ¹/8" from drawn line (**Fig. 1**).

Fig. 1

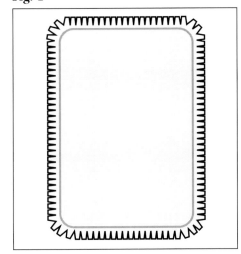

7. Center poster board piece on wrong side of fabric; **fuse** in place. Fold clipped edges of fabric to back of poster board; using a medium heat setting and a pressing cloth, **fuse** in place.
8. Glue covered poster board piece to inside of tray.

SUNNY DISH TOWELS
(Shown on page 52)

For each dish towel, you will need a woven cotton dish towel and 1 Silk Flower Appliqué (page 54).

1. Wash and dry dish towel several times to preshrink towel fabric as much as possible; press.
2. Fuse silk flower appliqué to dish towel.

TEA COZY (Shown on page 50)

For a 14" x 9" tea cozy, you will need one 16" x 22" fabric piece for cozy, one 16" x 22" fabric piece for lining, one 16" x 22" piece of fusible fleece, fabric for teapot and lid appliqués, print fabric for teapot decoration appliqués, fabric for binding and tab, paper-backed fusible web, 1/2"w paper-backed fusible web tape, tracing paper, one 5/8" button, embroidery floss, hot glue gun, and glue sticks.

1. Fuse fleece piece to wrong side of lining fabric piece. **Fuse** web to wrong side of cozy fabric piece; remove paper backing. **Fuse** wrong side of cozy fabric piece to fleece side of lining fabric piece.

2. Fold a piece of tracing paper in half and place fold along dashed line of tea cozy pattern. Trace pattern half; turn folded paper over and draw over traced lines. Unfold paper and cut out pattern.

3. Use pattern to cut 2 cozy pieces from fused fabric.

4. For binding, cut one 2 1/8" x 26" bias fabric strip and two 2 1/8" x 14 1/2" bias strips. Make 1/2"w **binding** from each fabric strip.

5. Insert bottom edge of 1 cozy piece into fold of one 14 1/2" long binding strip; **fuse** in place. Repeat for remaining cozy piece.

6. With lining sides facing, pin cozy pieces together. Beginning 1" from 1 end of binding strip and working on small sections at a time, insert raw edges of cozy pieces into fold of 26" long binding strip and **fuse**

in place (**Fig. 1**), being careful not to fuse ends of binding together. Open cozy and fold ends of binding to inside of cozy; **fuse** in place.

Fig. 1

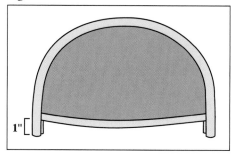

7. For tab, cut one 2 1/8" x 3 1/4" bias fabric strip. Make 1/2"w **binding** from fabric strip. **Fuse** folded edges of strip together. Fold 1 end of strip 1/4" to 1 side; glue in place. Fold remaining end of strip to overlap first end of strip; glue in place. Glue overlapped end of tab to center top on front of cozy.

8. Thread floss through button to resemble stitching. Glue floss ends to back of button. Glue button to tab.

9. For appliqués, **fuse** web to wrong sides of appliqué and print fabrics. Trace teapot and lid patterns onto tracing paper; cut out. Use patterns to cut appliqués from fabric. Cut desired motifs from print fabric. Remove paper backing. **Fuse** appliqués and motifs to front of cozy.

TEAPOT LID PATTERN

TEA COZY PATTERN

TEAPOT PATTERN

The projects on these pages require the use of the following techniques which are shown in **bold print** in the instructions. Please familiarize yourself with the General Instructions, pages 118 - 127, and these specific techniques before beginning the projects.

- Fusing (page 123)
- Making Binding (page 125)

57

For each place mat, you will need one 17¹⁄₂" x 22¹⁄₂" fabric piece for border, one 12¹⁄₂" x 17¹⁄₂" fabric piece for center, lightweight fusible interfacing, paper-backed fusible web, ¹⁄₂"w and ³⁄₈"w paper-backed fusible web tape, 1¹⁄₃ yds of ³⁄₈"w grosgrain ribbon, four ¹⁄₂" buttons, and fabric glue.

For each napkin and napkin tie, you will need a woven cotton dish towel, a large silk flower, 32" of grosgrain ribbon, wire cutters, hot glue gun, and glue sticks.

PLACE MAT

1. Fuse interfacing to wrong sides of border and center fabric pieces. **Fuse** web to wrong side of center piece. Do not remove paper backing.

2. Cut a 2¹⁄₂" square from each corner of border fabric piece as shown in **Fig. 1**.

Fig. 1

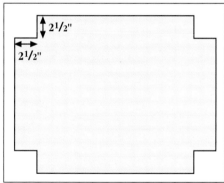

3. Remove paper backing from center fabric piece. **Fuse** center fabric piece to center on wrong side of border fabric piece.

4. Press 1 short edge of border fabric piece ¹⁄₂" to wrong side. **Fuse** ¹⁄₂"w web tape along pressed edge on wrong side of fabric piece. Do not remove paper backing. Press edge 2" to wrong side, covering edge of center fabric piece (**Fig. 2**). Unfold edge and remove paper backing. Refold edge and **fuse** in place. Repeat for remaining short edge of border fabric piece.

Fig. 2

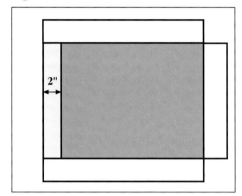

2"

5. Press 1 corner of 1 long edge of border fabric piece diagonally to wrong side as shown in **Fig. 3**; **fuse** ¹⁄₂"w web tape along diagonal edge (**Fig. 4**). Do not remove paper backing. Repeat for remaining 3 corners.

Fig. 3

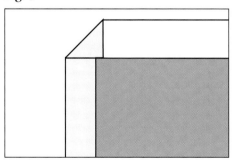

Fig. 4

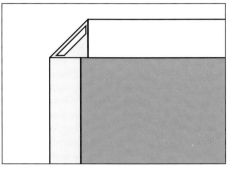

6. Press 1 remaining raw edge of border fabric piece ¹⁄₂" to wrong side. **Fuse** ¹⁄₂"w web tape along pressed edge on wrong side of fabric piece. Do not remove paper backing. Press edge 2" to wrong side, covering edge of center fabric piece. Unfold edge and remove paper backing from long and diagonal edges. Refold edge and **fuse** in place. Repeat for remaining raw edge of border fabric piece.

7. For ribbon trim, **fuse** ³⁄₈"w web tape to 1 side of ribbon; remove paper backing. Cut 1 length to fit along each inner edge of place mat border. **Fuse** in place.

8. Glue 1 button to each corner of ribbon trim.

NAPKIN AND NAPKIN TIE

1. For napkin, cut desired size square from towel. Fringe edges of fabric square ¹⁄₂".

2. For napkin tie, use wire cutters to trim stem close to base of flower. Glue center of ribbon to center back of flower. Tie ribbon around folded napkin.

"WELCOME" FLOORCLOTH

(Shown on page 51)

You will need a 24" x 36" piece of artist's canvas primed on 1 side, desired number of Silk Flower Appliqués (page 54), two 6" x 25" and two 6" x 37" fabric pieces for floorcloth border, 1"w paper-backed fusible web tape, 4"h lettering stencils, dark and light acrylic paint for lettering, ¹/₂"w foam brushes, paper towels, removable tape (optional), and satin-finish clear polyurethane spray.

1. For border pieces, make a 1" **single hem** along each long edge and 1 short edge of 1 border fabric piece. **Fuse** web tape along each hemmed edge on wrong side of border piece (**Fig. 1**). Do not remove paper backing. With wrong sides together, press border piece in half lengthwise; unfold. Remove paper backing. Refold border piece. Repeat for remaining border fabric pieces.

Fig. 1

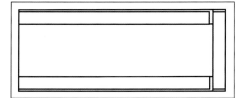

2. Place canvas, primed side up, with 1 long edge at top. With short unhemmed edge of border piece even with bottom edge of canvas, insert left edge of canvas into fold of 1 short border piece. Leaving top 12" of border piece unfused, **fuse** bottom 12" only of border piece to front and back of canvas (**Fig. 2**).

Fig. 2

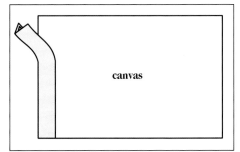

3. Referring to **Diagram** for placement of hemmed edges and fusing 1 border piece at a time, insert bottom, then right, then top edges of canvas into folds of remaining border pieces and **fuse** in place, being sure not to fuse unfused end of left border piece.

4. Finish border by inserting left edge of canvas into fold of unfused end of left border piece. **Fuse** in place.

5. For letter placement guideline, use a pencil and ruler to lightly draw a line on primed side of canvas 10" from bottom edge of floorcloth.

6. Using 1 foam brush and dark paint, follow Step 3 of **Stenciling** to center and stencil "WELCOME" along placement guideline. If desired, use paint to connect any gaps left in letters by stencils; allow to dry. Repeat to lightly stencil light paint over dark paint. Erase any visible pencil marks.

7. Arrange flower appliqués on canvas; **fuse** in place.

8. Allowing to dry between coats, apply 2 coats of polyurethane spray to front of floorcloth.

DIAGRAM

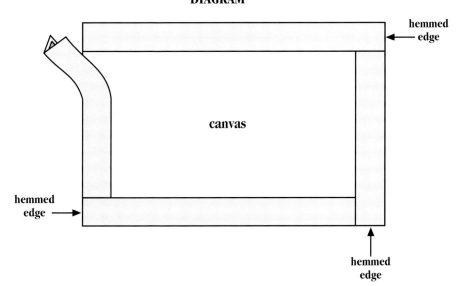

CAFÉ CURTAINS WITH LINED VALANCE

(Shown on page 49)

You will need a $1/2$" brass spring-tension rod for curtains, a $1/2$" spring-tension rod for valance, fabric for curtains and valance, fabric for valance lining, $1^{1}/8$" dia. brass clip-on café curtain rings, 1"w paper-backed fusible web tape, and 6"w strips of scrap fabric for "dressing" draperies (optional).

CURTAINS

1. Mount brass tension rod at desired height in window.

2. To determine width of each curtain fabric panel, measure length of mounted rod; multiply measurement by $1^{1}/2$. To determine length of each curtain fabric panel, measure from bottom of mounted rod to desired length; add $13^{1}/4$" for hems. Cut 2 fabric panels the determined measurements, **piecing fabric panels** as necessary.

3. Make a 3" **double hem** along top edge of each panel. Make a 1" **double hem** along each side edge of each panel. Make a 4" **double hem** along bottom edge of each panel.

4. Beginning and ending at top of side edges and spacing rings evenly, clip café rings to top of each panel approx. 8" apart. Hang curtains.

5. (**Note:** Have a professional dry cleaner "dress" pleats in curtains, or follow Step 5.) To "dress" or "set" pleats in curtains, pull curtains open to each side of window and loosely tie 1 or more fabric scraps around each curtain (**Fig. 1**); allow to hang for several days before removing scrap fabric.

Fig. 1

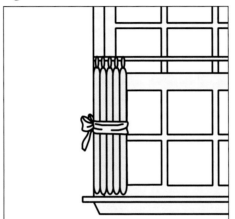

VALANCE

1. Mount tension rod in window $2^{1}/2$" from top of window.

2. To determine width of valance, measure length of mounted rod; multiply measurement by $2^{1}/2$. For valance, cut one $15^{1}/2$" long piece of curtain fabric the determined measurement, **piecing fabric panels** as necessary. Repeat to cut one 12" long piece of lining fabric the determined measurement (for lining) and one $3^{1}/2$" long piece of lining fabric the determined measurement (for casing).

3. Matching right sides, **fuse** 1 long edge (bottom) of valance fabric piece and 1 long edge of lining fabric piece together. Unfold fabrics and press seam allowance toward valance fabric.

4. Press each short edge of valance and lining fabric piece 1" to wrong side. **Fuse** an 11" length of web tape along each short edge of lining fabric piece (**Fig. 2**). Do not remove paper backing.

Fig. 2

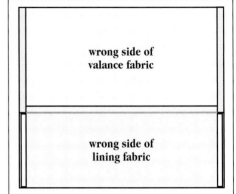

5. Press long raw edge of lining fabric to wrong side so that edge is $2^{1}/2$" below top edge of valance fabric (**Fig. 3**). Unfold edge and remove paper backing. Refold edge and **fuse** in place.

Fig. 3

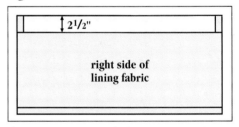

6. Referring to **Fig. 4**, **fuse** web tape along raw edge on wrong side of valance fabric and along raw edge on right side of lining fabric. Do not remove paper backing.

Fig. 4

CAFÉ CURTAINS WITH LINED VALANCE (Continued)

7. Press raw edge of valance fabric 2¹/₂" to wrong side, covering top edge of lining fabric (**Fig. 5**). Unfold edge and remove paper backing. Refold edge and **fuse** in place.

Fig. 5

8. For casing, press each short edge of casing fabric 1" to wrong side. **Fuse** web tape along each long raw edge on wrong side of casing; remove paper backing. Place casing wrong side down on lining side of valance with 1 long edge 1¹/₂" from top of valance (**Fig. 6**). **Fuse** casing in place.

Fig. 6

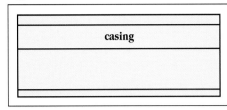

casing

9. Insert rod into casing and hang valance.

WATERING CAN (Shown on page 49)

You will need a galvanized tin watering can, spray primer, spray paint, acrylic paint for sponge painting, sponge piece, paper plate, silk flower with leaves, 26-gauge florist wire, wire cutters, fabric for can trim and streamers, grosgrain ribbon, ³/₈"w paper-backed fusible web tape, white vinegar, paper towels, hot glue gun, and glue sticks.

1. Wash watering can in hot soapy water (do not use lemon-scented soap). Rinse well. Rinse can in a solution of 1 part vinegar and 1 part water. Dry can completely.

2. Allowing to dry between coats, spray can with several light coats of primer, then spray paint.

3. To sponge paint can, pour a small amount of acrylic paint onto paper plate. Dip dampened sponge in paint and remove excess on a paper towel. Using a light stamping motion and reapplying paint to sponge as needed, sponge paint desired areas of can. Allow to dry.

4. For fabric trim on can, measure around area of can to be trimmed; add 1". Cut a 1"w bias strip of fabric the determined measurement. Press each long edge of strip ¹/₄" to wrong side. Press 1 end of strip ¹/₂" to wrong side. Beginning with unpressed end, glue strip around can. Repeat for remaining areas to be trimmed.

5. Use wire cutters to trim flower stem close to base of flower. Trim leaves from stem.

6. For fabric bow loops at top of flower, cut a 2¹/₄"x 24" bias strip of fabric. Make a ³/₈" **single hem** along each long edge of fabric strip. Cut strip into 3 equal lengths. Form each length into a loop and glue loops to back of flower.

7. Glue leaves to back of flower.

8. For curled streamers on flower, cut a 1¹/₄"w bias strip of fabric twice the desired length of streamers and make **wired fabric ribbon**. Fold wired fabric ribbon in half; glue fold of ribbon to back of flower. Curl ribbon ends.

9. Cut several lengths of grosgrain ribbon; glue lengths to back of flower to form streamers.

10. To secure flower to can, glue the center of a length of grosgrain ribbon to back of flower as shown in **Fig. 1**. Tie ribbon around handle of can.

Fig. 1

ROSY HAVEN

Lovely reminders of summer's delicate beauty, blushing roses transform this bed and bath into a delightful garden. Fabrics in soft florals and stripes create the inviting atmosphere, and pretty shades of pink, green, and white enhance the mood. Ribbons, lace, and other dainty trimmings add a feminine touch. To dress up the bed, we used simple techniques such as bringing new life to an old comforter with a beribboned duvet cover and making matching pillow shams. The three different window treatments in this section are all incredibly easy — here, the curtains are puddled for a fresh look that also allows you to skip the chore of obtaining precise measurements. Draped over the rod, a Battenberg lace tablecloth doubles as a valance and shade. A fabric-covered mat and bow for a framed print are examples of how little touches can help tie your whole room together. In a rosy haven such as this, your cares and worries are sure to slip away, allowing you to indulge in quiet reflection and sweet dreams of days to come.

Shirred Balloon Shade, page 78
Covered Vanity Table, page 71
Candlestick Lamps, page 68
Chair Seat Cover, page 72

A rosy fabric skirt topped with a Battenberg lace tablecloth dresses up an inexpensive unfinished vanity table (opposite). The dainty bows are wired ribbon that's surprisingly easy to make. An old chair can be made to match with a coordinating seat cover secured with bows. Casting a warm glow, candlestick lamps are trimmed with shirred fabric and matching floral motifs. The graceful balloon shade presents a charming view.

Fabric-covered boxes (left) make pretty and practical storage containers for feminine notions. Decorative pillows (below) feature ribbon, lace, and flowers cut from print fabric. The floral pillow shams are lovely accents.

*B*ringing a summery garden feeling to the bathroom, a flowery shower curtain (opposite) is topped with a beribboned valance made from a cutwork table runner. A pretty fabric-covered wastebasket and a lacy bench cover are decidedly feminine accents.

A pink-and-white striped valance (right) adds a soft touch to a window, and a floral tissue box cover (below) is an attractive addition to the bath or dressing room.

Pouf Valance, page 79
Tissue Box Cover, page 73

Shower Curtain with Cutwork Valance, page 72
Covered Wastebasket, page 73
Covered Bench, page 79

BATTENBERG LACE PILLOW

(Shown on page 65)

For a 21" x 15" pillow, you will need two 22" x 16" fabric pieces for pillow, an approx. 14$\frac{1}{2}$"w Battenberg lace-trimmed tea towel, 2 yds of $\frac{7}{8}$"w satin ribbon, $\frac{1}{2}$"w paper-backed fusible web tape, polyester fiberfill, and 2 small safety pins (optional).

1. Measuring from lace-trimmed end of tea towel, cut a 10" length from towel.
2. For pillow front, **fuse** web tape along raw edge on wrong side of towel piece. Remove paper backing. Matching wrong side of towel piece to right side of 1 pillow fabric piece (front), center raw edge of towel piece along 1 long edge of pillow fabric piece; **fuse** in place.
3. Make **pillow** from pillow front and remaining fabric piece (back).
4. Cut ribbon in half. Tie 1 ribbon length into a bow around each top corner of pillow; trim ends. If desired, use a safety pin to pin each bow in place.

CANDLESTICK LAMPS (Shown on page 64)

For each lamp, you will need a candlestick lamp, fabric and $\frac{1}{4}$"w satin ribbon to cover lamp, a 1$\frac{1}{2}$"w bias strip of fabric and $\frac{3}{8}$"w paper-backed fusible web tape for trim on shade, print fabric for appliqués on shade, paper-backed fusible web, fabric glue, and a rubber band.

1. For fabric to cover lamp, measure length of area to be covered (**Fig. 1**); multiply measurement by 2. Measure around area to be covered (**Fig. 2**); add 1". Cut a strip of fabric the determined measurements. Cut 2 lengths of ribbon the same length as 1 short edge of fabric strip.

Fig. 1   **Fig. 2**

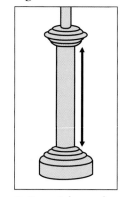 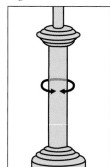

2. Press 1 long edge of fabric strip $\frac{1}{4}$" to wrong side and glue in place; allow to dry.
3. To cover lamp, apply a thin line of glue along $\frac{1}{3}$ of hemmed edge on wrong side of fabric strip (**Fig. 3**).

Fig. 3

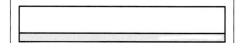

4. Wrap strip loosely around lamp, overlapping glued area $\frac{1}{4}$" over remaining long edge (**Fig. 4**). Use rubber band to hold excess fabric at top of lamp. Allow to dry. Carefully push glued area toward bottom of lamp and repeat to glue second $\frac{1}{3}$ of fabric strip, and then final $\frac{1}{3}$ of fabric strip.

Fig. 4

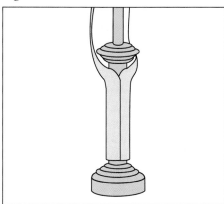

5. Wrap 1 ribbon length tightly around top edge of fabric, covering raw edge; glue to secure. Repeat to glue remaining ribbon around bottom raw edge of fabric.
6. Distribute gathers of fabric evenly along base.
7. For trim along top edge of lampshade, measure around top of shade; add 1". Make $\frac{1}{2}$"w **fabric trim** the determined measurement from fabric strip. Press 1 end of trim $\frac{1}{2}$" to wrong side. Beginning with unpressed end at seam of shade, glue trim along top edge of shade. Repeat for trim along bottom edge of shade.
8. For appliqués on shade, **fuse** web to wrong side of print fabric. Cut desired motifs from fabric. **Fuse** appliqués to shade.

For each covered box, you will need a papier mâché box with lid (we used heart-shaped, round, and hexagonal boxes), fabric to cover box, paper-backed fusible web, and fabric glue.

For trim on each box, you may also need ribbons (we used moiré, organdy, wired silk, and satin ribbons), a Battenberg lace doily to fit on lid of box, a cutwork napkin or handkerchief, silk flowers, florist wire, hot glue gun, and glue sticks.

COVERING BOX

1. Fuse web to wrong side of fabric.

2. For fabric strip to cover sides of box, measure height of box; add 2". Measure around side of box; add 1". Cut a strip of fabric the determined measurements. For fabric piece to cover bottom of box, use a pencil to draw around bottom of box on wrong side of fabric. Cut out shape 1/8" inside drawn line. For fabric piece to cover box lid, use pencil to draw around top of lid on wrong side of fabric. Cut out shape 2" outside drawn line.

3. To cover side of box, fold 1 short edge of fabric strip 1/2" to wrong side and **fuse** in place. Beginning with unpressed edge, center strip on side of box and wrap strip around box; **fuse** in place. Use fabric glue to secure fabric at overlap.

4. At 1" intervals, clip fabric extending beyond top and bottom of box to 1/8" from box edges. Fold clipped edges at top of box to inside of box; **fuse** in place. **Fuse** clipped edges at bottom to bottom of box. Use fabric glue to secure clipped edges at overlap.

5. To cover bottom of box, center and **fuse** small fabric shape to bottom of box.

6. (Note: Follow Step 6 to cover heart-shaped or round box lid. Follow Step 7 to cover hexagonal, square, or rectangular box lid.) For heart-shaped or round box lid, center and **fuse** large fabric shape to top of lid. At 1" intervals, clip fabric extending beyond top of lid to 1/8" from top of lid. **Fuse** clipped edges to side of lid. Fold remaining fabric to inside of lid; **fuse** in place.

7. For hexagonal, square, or rectangular box lid, center and **fuse** large fabric shape to top of lid. Clip fabric extending beyond top of lid to 1/8" from top of lid at each corner (**Fig. 1**). **Fuse** alternate clipped edges to side of lid (**Fig. 2**). Fold corners of remaining clipped edges to wrong side and **fuse** in place (**Fig. 3**); **fuse** edges to side of lid. Fold remaining fabric to inside of lid; **fuse** in place. Use fabric glue to secure fabric at corners.

Fig. 1

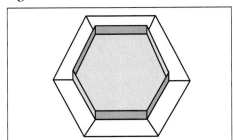

Fig. 2

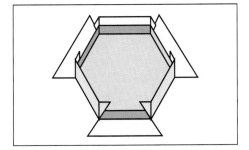

Fig. 3

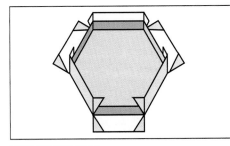

TRIMMING BOX

1. (Note: Use the following steps as suggestions to trim your box. Use fabric glue for gluing unless otherwise indicated.) For ribbon on side of box lid, measure around side of lid; add 1/2". Using the determined measurement, cut a length from ribbon same width as side of lid. Glue ribbon to side of lid.

2. For doily on lid, center and glue doily to top of lid.

3. For napkin corner on lid, glue 1 corner of napkin to top of lid. Trim remainder of napkin to 1/2" from top of lid. At 1" intervals, clip raw edge of napkin corner to within 1/4" of top of lid. Glue clipped edges to side of lid. Measure around side of lid; add 1/2". Cut a length of narrow ribbon the determined measurement. Glue ribbon to side of lid, covering raw edge of napkin corner.

4. For nosegay on lid, wire a small bunch of flowers together. Tie lengths of ribbons together into a bow. Hot glue bow to flowers, covering wire. Hot glue nosegay to box.

FLORAL APPLIQUÉ PILLOW

(Shown on page 65)

For a 15¹/₂" square pillow, you will need two 17¹/₂" fabric squares for pillow, floral print fabric for appliqué(s), an 11" fabric square for appliqué background, two 2" x 11" and two 2" x 13" fabric strips for trim around background, paper-backed fusible web, 1"w paper-backed fusible web tape, 2¹/₄ yds of ¹/₄"w satin ribbon, four ⁷/₈" four-hole buttons, fabric glue, and polyester fiberfill.

1. Fuse web to wrong sides of appliqué and background fabric pieces. Remove paper backing. Center and **fuse** background fabric piece to right side of 1 pillow fabric square (front). Cut out desired motif(s) from appliqué fabric. Arrange motif(s) on background fabric piece; **fuse** in place.

2. For trim around background, press long edges of each 11" fabric strip and long and short edges of each 13" fabric strip ¹/₂" to wrong side. **Fuse** web tape to wrong side of each pressed trim strip. Centering trim strips over raw edges, arrange 11" strips along side edges and remaining strips along top and bottom edges of background; **fuse** in place.

3. For ribbon and button trim, refer to **Fig. 1** to thread 1 button onto ribbon, positioning button at center of ribbon. Glue button to center of lower left corner of trim. Glue ribbon lengths extending from button along center of fabric trim to adjacent corners. Thread another button onto each end of ribbon (**Fig. 1**) and glue buttons to centers of corners. Continue gluing ribbon lengths along fabric trim to top right corner. Threading ribbon ends from back of remaining button, thread each end of ribbon diagonally through remaining button. Tie ribbon ends into a double-loop bow under button; trim ends. Glue bow and button to corner.

Fig. 1

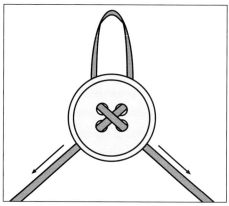

4. Make **pillow** from pillow front and remaining fabric piece (back).

COVERED PICTURE MAT

(Shown on page 63)

You will need a mat to fit desired picture and frame, a fabric piece slightly larger than mat, and paper-backed fusible web.

1. Fuse web to wrong side of fabric piece; do not remove paper backing.
2. Use a pencil to draw around mat and mat opening on paper backing side of fabric piece. Cut out fabric along outer lines. Referring to **Fig. 1**, cut opening in fabric 1" inside inner lines; at corners of opening, clip fabric to ¹/₈" from drawn lines. Remove paper backing.

Fig. 1

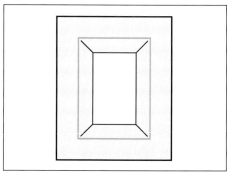

3. Matching outer edges, place fabric piece right side up on front of mat. Being careful to fuse fabric over mat only, **fuse** fabric to mat. Turn mat over. Fold inner edges of fabric over edges to back of mat and **fuse** in place (**Fig. 2**).

Fig. 2

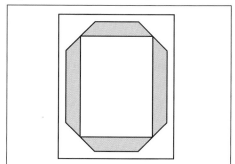

RIBBON HANGER FOR PICTURE FRAME

(Shown on page 63)

For an approx. 1 yd long hanger with 8¹/₂"w bow, you will need desired picture in frame, two 3¹/₂" x 45" fabric strips, ¹/₂"w paper-backed fusible web tape, 26-gauge florist wire, wire cutters, two 1" safety pins, hot glue gun, and glue sticks.

1. Make **wired fabric ribbon** from each fabric strip.
2. Make a **wired ribbon bow** with 11" streamers from 1 ribbon length.
3. For ribbon hanger, press corners of 1 end (top) of remaining ribbon length diagonally to wrong side to form a point (**Fig. 1**); use small pieces of web tape to **fuse** corners in place.

Fig. 1

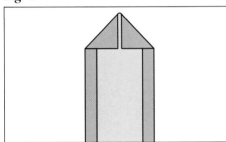

4. Using 1 safety pin on wrong side of ribbon hanger, pin bow 3" from top (**Fig. 2**). Use remaining pin to pin hanger on back of frame to right side of ribbon below bow. Cut a V-shaped notch in end of ribbon below frame. Hang ribbon hanger from top safety pin.

Fig. 2

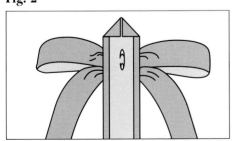

COVERED VANITY TABLE (Shown on page 64)

You will need an unfinished plywood vanity table made for covering, muslin fabric and fusible fleece for padded tabletop, fabric for skirt, fabric for bows, an oval or rectangular Battenberg lace-trimmed tablecloth at least 12" larger on all sides than tabletop, ¹/₂"w paper-backed fusible web tape, 1"w fusible double-cord shirring tape, ³/₄"w hook and loop fastener tape, 1" safety pins, hot glue gun, glue sticks, 26-gauge florist wire, and wire cutters.

1. To pad tabletop, cut a piece of fleece 1" larger on all sides than tabletop. Cut a piece of muslin 2" larger on all sides than tabletop. Center and **fuse** fleece to muslin. Center tabletop, top side down, on fleece side of muslin. Alternating sides and pulling muslin until smooth, glue edges of muslin to bottom of tabletop.
2. For length of fabric piece for skirt, measure from top of table to floor; add 3¹/₄". For width of fabric piece, measure around edge of tabletop; multiply measurement by 2¹/₂. Cut a piece of fabric the determined measurements, **piecing fabric panels** as necessary.
3. Make a ¹/₂" **double hem** along each short edge of fabric piece. Make a 1¹/₂" **double hem** along 1 long edge (bottom) of fabric piece. Make a ¹/₂" **single hem** along top edge of fabric piece.
4. Cut a length of shirring tape same length as top edge of fabric piece. **Fuse** tape along top edge on wrong side of fabric piece. Pull cords of shirring tape, gathering fabric piece to fit around edge of tabletop; securely knot cords and trim ends.

5. Measure around edge of tabletop. Cut a length of hook and loop fastener tape the determined measurement. Glue hook side of tape along edge of tabletop. Glue loop side of tape over gathered shirring tape on wrong side of skirt.
6. Attach skirt to tabletop.
7. For topper, center tablecloth on tabletop.
8. For each gathered area along edge of topper, refer to **Fig. 1** and use a safety pin on wrong side of topper to gather topper from edge of fabric to edge of tabletop.

Fig. 1

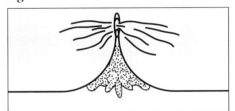

9. For each bow, cut a 4" x 48" fabric strip, **piecing fabric strips** as necessary. Make **wired fabric ribbon** from fabric strip. Make a **wired ribbon bow** with 12" streamers from ribbon length.
10. Glue bows over gathered areas of topper.

CHAIR SEAT COVER

(Shown on page 64)

You will need a straight-back chair, fabrics for cover and ties, 1/2"w paper-backed fusible web tape, craft paper or newspaper, and two 1" safety pins.

1. For pattern, measure seat of chair; use a ruler to draw shape of seat on craft paper. Add 7" to front and to each side and 1" to back (**Fig. 1**). Cut out pattern.

Fig. 1

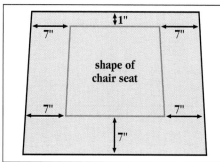

2. Use pattern to cut a piece from cover fabric.

3. Make 1/2" **double hems** along all edges of fabric piece.

4. For ties, cut four 3" x 48" strips from tie fabric, **piecing fabric strips** as necessary. Trim ends of each strip at an angle. Make 1/2" **single hems** along ends and then along long edges of each strip, trimming excess fabric at corners.

5. With back edge of cover centered along back edge of chair seat, place cover on seat. Use pins to mark placement of each upright of chair back along back edge of cover (**Fig. 2**). Remove cover from seat.

Fig. 2

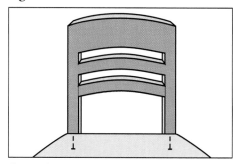

6. Matching right side of tie to wrong side of cover and matching center of 1 long edge of tie to back edge of cover, use a safety pin to pin 1 tie to hem of cover at each pin mark (**Fig. 3**).

Fig. 3

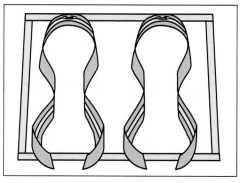

7. Place cover on chair. Tie back ties into bows around uprights of chair back. Tie 1 remaining tie around each front corner of cover and chair leg.

SHOWER CURTAIN WITH CUTWORK VALANCE

(Shown on page 67)

For a standard shower curtain (72" square), you will need a 78"w x 82"l fabric piece (see **Piecing Fabric Panels**), an 18" x 72" cutwork table runner for valance, 1 1/2"w paper-backed fusible web tape, shower curtain liner, dimensional fabric paint in squeeze bottle, shower curtain rings (ours were purchased with fabric covers), 12 yds of 7/8"w satin ribbon, and a 1/4" hole punch.

1. For curtain, make a 1 1/2" **double hem** along long edges and 1 short edge (top) of fabric piece; make a 3 1/2" **double hem** along bottom edge.

2. For eyelets for curtain rings, place shower curtain liner and curtain wrong sides together with liner 1/4" below top edge of curtain.

3. Use a pencil to mark a dot on curtain at center of each eyelet in liner. Use hole punch to punch a hole at each dot. Use dimensional paint to paint along edge of each hole on right side of curtain; allow to dry. Paint along edge of each hole on wrong side of curtain; allow to dry.

4. For eyelets along top edge of valance, center curtain right side up on right side of table runner with top edge of curtain even with 1 long edge (top) of table runner and repeat Step 3.

5. Use rings to hang liner, shower curtain, and valance on rod.

6. Cut ribbon into 1 yd lengths. Tie 1 ribbon length into a bow around front of each ring; trim ends.

TISSUE BOX COVER (Shown on page 66)

You will need a plastic tissue box cover, fabrics for cover and bow, 1/2"w fusible single-cord shirring tape, 3/8"w and 1/2"w paper-backed fusible web tape, silk flowers, spray adhesive, hot glue gun, and glue sticks.

1. To cover tissue box cover, use a pencil to draw around top of tissue box cover, including opening, on wrong side of fabric. Referring to **Fig. 1**, cut out shape 1" from pencil lines; at 1/2" intervals, clip edges of opening and edges at corners of fabric to 1/8" from drawn lines.

Fig. 1

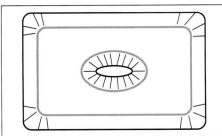

2. Apply spray adhesive to wrong side of fabric piece; center and smooth fabric piece onto top of tissue box cover. Fold clipped edges of fabric at opening over edges to inside; smooth in place. Smooth remaining edges onto side of cover. If necessary, hot glue clipped edges to inside of cover to secure.

3. To cover side of tissue box cover, measure around side of cover at widest point; multiply measurement by 2 1/2. Measure height of cover; add 1 1/2". Cut a strip of fabric the determined measurements, **piecing fabric strips** as necessary. Cut 2 lengths of shirring tape same length as fabric strip.

4. Fuse 1 length of shirring tape 5/8" from each long edge of fabric strip.

5. Make a 3/8" **single hem** along each long edge of fabric strip, overlapping edge of fabric 1/8" over edge of shirring tape. Use a pin to mark center of each long edge of strip.

6. Gathering fabric evenly on each side of pins, pull cords in shirring tape, gathering fabric strip to fit around sides of cover with ends overlapping 3/4". Distribute gathers evenly along fabric strip. Securely knot cords and trim ends. Make a 3/8" **single hem** along 1 end of fabric strip.

7. (Note: Use hot glue for gluing in remaining steps.) Beginning with unhemmed end of gathered strip at center back of cover, glue top edge of strip along top edge of cover, gluing shirring tape only to cover and leaving ruffle at edge loose. Repeat to glue bottom edge of strip along bottom edge of cover. Glue ends of fabric strip together.

8. For bow, cut a 2 1/8" x 12" bias strip of fabric. Use 1/2"w web tape to make 3/4"w **fabric trim** from bias strip. Form trim into a figure 8, overlapping ends 1/2" (**Fig. 2**); glue to secure. Glue flowers to front of bow.

Fig. 2

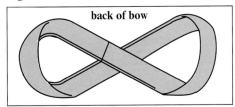
back of bow

9. Glue bow to center front of cover.

COVERED WASTEBASKET (Shown on page 67)

You will need a plastic wastebasket with straight sides, fabric for cover, fabric for bow and trim, 1"w fusible double-cord shirring tape, 3/8"w and 1/2"w paper-backed fusible web tape, silk flowers, hot glue gun, and glue sticks.

1. To cover wastebasket, measure around side of wastebasket at widest point; multiply measurement by 2 1/2. Measure height of wastebasket; add 3". Cut a piece of fabric the determined measurements, **piecing fabric panels** as necessary. Cut 2 lengths of shirring tape same length as fabric piece.

2. Follow Steps 4 - 6 of **Tissue Box Cover** to finish wastebasket cover.

3. With top edge of cover extending 1/4" above top edge of wastebasket, follow Step 7 of **Tissue Box Cover** to glue cover to wastebasket (cover will be full).

4. For trim, measure around side of wastebasket 1" below top; add 1". Cut a 2 1/8"w bias strip of fabric the determined measurement. Use 1/2"w web tape to make 3/4"w **fabric trim** from bias strip. Beginning at center front of wastebasket, glue trim around wastebasket approx. 1" below top, overlapping ends 1/2" and trimming excess.

5. For bow, follow Step 8 of **Tissue Box Cover**. Glue bow to wastebasket over ends of trim.

You will need a duvet (comforter); fabrics for top, back, and flap of cover; fabric and 3/8" dia. cotton cord for welting; 1"w paper-backed fusible web tape; dimensional fabric paint in squeeze bottle; 5 1/3 yds of 1 1/2"w satin ribbon for ties; four 1" safety pins; small sharp scissors; fabric glue; and spring-type clothespins.

1. (**Note:** Duvet cover is made slightly smaller than duvet to make covered duvet appear full.) For cover top and back, measure width and length of duvet; add 3" to length. Cut 2 fabric pieces the determined measurements, **piecing fabric panels** as necessary.

2. Make a 1" **double hem** along top edge of cover top and back fabric pieces.

3. For welting, measure 1 side, bottom, and remaining side edge of cover top fabric piece; add 4". Cut a 3 1/4"w strip of fabric the determined measurement, **piecing fabric strips** as necessary. Cut a length of cord same length as fabric strip. Make **welting** from fabric strip and cord.

4. **Fuse** web tape along raw edge on 1 side of welting seam allowance. Remove paper backing. Beginning 1" from 1 end of welting and matching long raw edge of welting to raw edge of cover top, **fuse** welting along side and bottom edges on right side of cover top, clipping seam allowance of welting at corners. Trim remaining end of welting 1" beyond top edge of cover top.

5. To finish each end of welting, pull apart 3" of fused edges at end of welting; trim 1" from end of cord (**Fig. 1**). Fold end of welting fabric over end of cord (**Fig. 2**); **fuse** welting back together. If necessary, glue ends of welting fabric together; secure with a clothespin until glue is dry.

Fig. 1

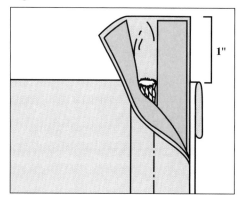

Fig. 2

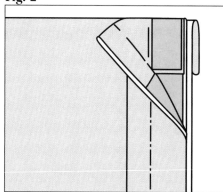

6. **Fuse** web tape along raw edge on remaining side of welting seam allowance. Remove paper backing. With cover top and back right sides together, **fuse** edges of top and back together. If necessary, use fabric glue at top corners to reinforce seams; secure with clothespins until glue is dry.

7. Do not clip seam allowance at corners. Turn cover right side out and carefully push corners outward, making sure seam allowances lie flat. Press edges of cover close to welting.

8. For flap, measure width of finished duvet cover excluding welting; add 2". Cut 2 strips of fabric 12"w by the determined measurement. Omitting Step 4, follow **Making a Pillow** to make flap from fabric strips.

9. To attach flap to cover, **fuse** web tape along top edge on right side of back of cover; **fuse** web tape along 1 long edge on 1 side of flap. Remove paper backing. Overlapping taped edges 1", place taped edges together and **fuse** flap to back of cover (**Fig. 3**).

Fig. 3

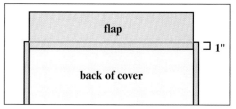

10. For holes for ribbon ties, refer to **Diagram**, page 75, and use a pencil to draw 4 evenly spaced 1" long lines 1" from top edge on front of flap. Use small scissors to cut through front and back of flap along pencil lines. Use dimensional paint to paint around each hole on front of flap (**Fig. 4**); allow to dry. Paint around each hole on back of flap; allow to dry.

Fig. 4

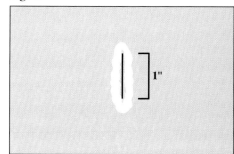

11. Insert duvet in cover.

12. For ties, cut ribbon into four equal lengths. Fold flap over opening to front of cover. Use a pin to mark placement of each tie on cover front through holes in flap. Unfold flap. With pins on inside of cover, safety pin center of 1 ribbon length at each mark on cover. To close cover, insert 1 end of each ribbon length through 1 hole in flap. Tie ribbons into bows; trim ends.

WELTED DUVET COVER (Continued)

DIAGRAM

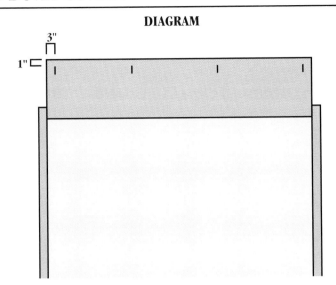

DUST RUFFLE (Shown on page 63)

This dust ruffle is designed to be 1 continuous ruffle. Ruffle may be made in 3 pieces to allow for corner posts of footboard.

You will need fabric for ruffle, a fitted sheet, 3/4"w paper-backed fusible web tape, 3"w pregathered lace trim, 1"w fusible double-cord shirring tape, 1" safety pins, and scrap cardboard.

1. Measure around sides of bed; multiply measurement by 2 1/2. **Measure** from top of box springs to floor; subtract 3/4". Cut a piece of fabric the determined measurements, **piecing fabric panels** as necessary. Cut a length of lace 1 1/2" shorter than length of fabric piece. Cut a length of shirring tape 3" shorter than length of fabric piece.
2. Make a 3/4" **double hem** along each short edge of fabric piece. Make a 3/4" **single hem** along each long edge of fabric piece.

3. For lace trim, make a 3/4" **single hem** along each end of lace. **Fuse** web tape along 1 long edge (bottom) on wrong side of fabric piece. Remove paper backing. With right side of lace facing wrong side of fabric piece and straight edge of lace along top edge of web, **fuse** lace to fabric piece.
4. Fuse shirring tape along top edge on wrong side of fabric piece. Use a pin to mark center of top edge.
5. Gathering fabric evenly on each side of pin, pull cords in shirring tape, gathering ruffle to fit around sides of bed. Distribute gathers evenly along ruffle. Knot cords and wrap excess around a small piece of cardboard.
6. Place sheet on box springs. Use safety pins to pin top edge of ruffle along top edge of sheet. Pin excess cords to sheet under ruffle.

EYELET LACE PILLOW
(Shown on page 65)

For a 16 1/2" x 12 1/2" pillow, you will need two 17 1/2" x 13 1/2" fabric pieces for pillow, two 17 1/2" lengths of 6"w flat eyelet lace trim, two 18" lengths of ribbon to thread through trim (optional), 1/2"w paper-backed fusible web tape, and polyester fiberfill.

1. If desired, thread 1 ribbon length through each length of eyelet trim.
2. For pillow front, **fuse** web tape along raw edges on wrong side of each eyelet trim length. Matching raw edges, **fuse** 1 trim length along each long edge on right side of 1 pillow fabric piece (front).
3. Make **pillow** from pillow front and remaining fabric piece (back).

For each sham with 3" flange, you will need a pillow, fabrics for sham and trim, ³/₄"w and 1"w paper-backed fusible web tape, fabric glue, 6" of ³/₄"w hook and loop fastener tape, and hook and loop fastener adhesive.

1. For sham top, measure width and length of pillow; add 6¹/₂" to each measurement. Cut 1 fabric piece the determined measurement (for a standard 26" x 20" pillow, fabric piece should be 32¹/₂" x 26¹/₂").

2. For sham back, divide width of sham top by 2 and add 3¹/₂". Cut 2 fabric pieces same length as sham top by the determined measurement (for a standard 26" x 20" pillow, fabric pieces should be 19³/₄" x 26¹/₂".)

3. To hem opening edges of sham back, position sham top wrong side up. Matching edges, arrange sham back fabric pieces right side up on sham top with pieces overlapping 7" at center. Mark each overlapping edge with a pin. Make a ³/₄" **double hem** along marked edge of each back fabric piece.

4. On right side of each sham back fabric piece, **fuse** ³/₄"w web tape along raw edges. Remove paper backing.

*The projects on these pages require the use of the following techniques which are shown in **bold print** in the instructions. Please familiarize yourself with the General Instructions, pages 118 - 127, and these specific techniques before beginning the projects.*

- *Fusing (page 123)*
- *Piecing Fabric Strips (page 123)*
- *Making a Single Hem (page 124)*
- *Making a Double Hem (page 124)*
- *Making Fabric Trim (page 125)*

5. Position sham top right side up. Matching raw edges, place sham back pieces wrong side up on sham top with hemmed edges overlapping at center. **Fuse** sham back pieces to sham top.

6. On wrong side of sham top, use a pencil to draw a line 3" from each edge. **Fuse** ³/₄"w web tape just inside lines as shown in **Fig. 1**. Remove paper backing.

Fig. 1

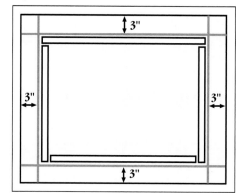

7. Do not clip seam allowance at corners. Turn sham right side out and carefully push corners outward, making sure seam allowances lie flat. Press edges of sham only. For flange, carefully **fuse** sham top and back together along remainder of web tape.

8. To relieve stress on seams at back opening, cut hook and loop fastener tape in half. Referring to **Fig. 2**, apply 1 length of fastener tape at top and bottom of back opening.

Fig. 2

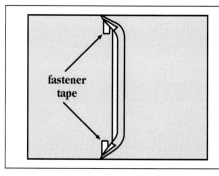

fastener tape

9. For trim on sham, measure around edges of sham. Cut a 4¹/₈"w strip of trim fabric the determined measurement, **piecing fabric strips** as necessary. Use 1"w web tape to make 1¹/₂"w **fabric trim** from fabric strip.

10. **Fuse** ³/₄" web tape along each long edge on wrong side of trim. Remove paper backing. Begin at 1 corner of sham and **fuse** trim 1¹/₂" from edges of sham along inner edge of flange (**Fig. 3**). At each corner of sham, refer to **Fig. 4** to fold trim for mitered corner and **Fig. 5** to **fuse** mitered corner in place. At last corner, stop fusing 3" from corner and trim end of trim even with first end of trim (**Fig. 6**). Fold end of trim diagonally to wrong side to form miter and finish fusing. Use fabric glue at corners of trim to secure miters.

Fig. 3

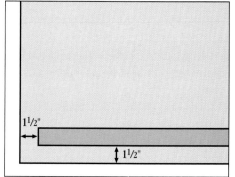

1¹/₂"

1¹/₂"

SINGLE-FLANGE PILLOW SHAMS (Continued)

Fig. 4

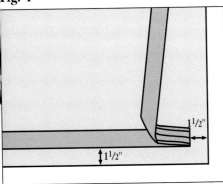

Fig. 5

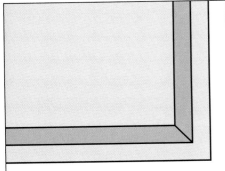

Fig. 6

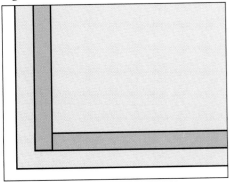

CURTAINS WITH BATTENBERG LACE VALANCE AND SHADE

(Shown on page 63)

You will need a 1¼" dia. decorator curtain rod, fabric for curtains (we used 1 full width of 54"w fabric for each panel), a rectangular Battenberg lace tablecloth for valance and shade, 1½"w paper-backed fusible web tape, 1" safety pins, ribbons (we used 1½"w wired moiré and 3"w organdy ribbons), silk flowers, and 2 cup hooks or tacks.

1. Mount curtain rod.
2. For fabric panels, measure from top of rod to desired length; add 10½" for casing and hem (for enough length to allow panels to "puddle" on floor, add an extra 20" to rod-to-floor measurement). Cut 2 lengths of fabric the determined measurement.
3. For each panel, make 1½" **double hem**s along both long edges and 1 short edge (bottom) of fabric length. Make a 1½" **single hem** along top edge of fabric length.
4. For casing at top of each panel, **fuse** web tape along top edge on wrong side. Do not remove paper backing. Press edge 6" to wrong side. Unfold edge and remove paper backing. Refold edge and **fuse** in place.
5. Remove rod from window and insert through casing of each panel; hang curtains.
6. For each tieback, tie ribbons together into a bow around panel; trim ends. Use a cup hook or tack to attach tieback to wall behind bow. Use a safety pin to pin a flower at center of bow.

7. If "puddle" effect is desired, tuck hemmed edge of fabric under at floor and arrange folds. It may be helpful to use a rubber band to gather end of panel before tucking it under.
8. To determine width of tablecloth needed for valance and shade, measure length of curtain rod between finials. To determine length of tablecloth needed, measure desired length of valance and desired length of shade from top of rod; add measurements together and add 1". Tablecloth should be as close as possible to these measurements.
9. Drape tablecloth over rod, adjusting tablecloth from front to back to achieve desired length of valance and shade.
10. For each gathered area along edge of valance and shade, refer to **Fig. 1** and use a safety pin on wrong side of valance or shade to gather fabric as desired.

Fig. 1

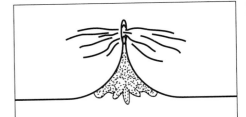

SHIRRED BALLOON SHADE (Shown on page 64)

These instructions are for windows measuring up to 72" wide. Although the length of the shade is adjustable, the shade is designed to be stationary when hung.

You will need a 2¹/₂"w Continental® curtain rod, fabric for shade, ¹/₂"w and 1"w paper-backed fusible web tape, ¹/₂"w fusible balloon shade tape, shade cord, 3"w pregathered lace trim, scrap cardboard, and tissue paper (optional).

1. Mount curtain rod.
2. To determine width of each fabric panel for shade, measure length of curtain rod; multiply measurement by 2¹/₂ and divide by 3. To determine length of each panel, measure from top of rod to bottom of window frame; add 11" for header, casing, and hem. If fullness is desired when shade is fully extended, add an extra 18" to measurement. Cut 3 fabric panels the determined measurements, **piecing fabric panels** as necessary.
3. Use 1"w web tape to **piece fabric panels** together along long edges to form 1 fabric piece.
4. Make a 1" **double hem** along side edges of fabric piece.
5. To determine length of balloon shade tape, subtract 14¹/₂" from length of fabric piece. With first ring of each tape length 1" from 1 end (bottom), cut 4 lengths of balloon shade tape the determined measurement.
6. Beginning 2¹/₂" from bottom edge of fabric piece, **fuse** 1 length of balloon shade tape ¹/₂" from each side edge of fabric piece and 1 length along center of each seam between panels (see **Diagram**), making sure rings are aligned.

7. Make a 1" **double hem** along bottom edge of fabric piece. Make a 1" **single hem** along top edge of fabric piece.
8. For header and casing, **fuse** 1"w web tape along top edge on wrong side of shade; **fuse** another length 3" below first length. Do not remove paper backing. Press edge of shade 6" to wrong side; unfold. Remove paper backing from both lengths of web tape. Refold edge and **fuse** in place.
9. For lace trim, cut a length of lace 1" longer than width of shade. Make a ¹/₂" **single hem** along each end of lace. **Fuse** ¹/₂"w web tape along bottom edge on wrong side of shade. Remove paper backing. With right side of lace facing wrong side of shade

and straight edge of lace along top edge of web tape, **fuse** lace to shade.
10. For cords, cut 4 lengths of shade cord same length as shade. For each length of balloon shade tape, knot 1 cord to bottom ring and thread cord through rings to top of tape.
11. Remove rod from window and insert through casing at top of shade; hang shade. Pull cords to raise bottom of shade to desired height. Knot cords to top rings on balloon shade tape. Wrap excess cord around small pieces of cardboard and pin to back of casing.
12. Arrange poufs in shade, stuffing with tissue paper if desired to maintain shape.

DIAGRAM

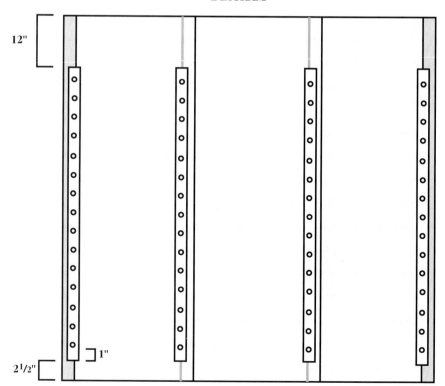

POUF VALANCE (Shown on page 66)

You will need two ½" spring-tension rods or 2 conventional curtain rods, fabric for valance, ½"w and 1"w paper-backed fusible web tape, 5"w flat eyelet trim, and tissue paper (optional).

1. Allowing 2" for header, position top rod as desired. Position second rod 5" above desired finished length of valance including eyelet trim (see **Diagram**; we positioned our rods approx. 10" apart for our 17" long valance). For tension rods, use a pencil to mark placement of rods in window.

2. To determine width of fabric piece, measure length of 1 rod; multiply measurement by 2½. To determine length of fabric piece, measure from top of first rod to bottom of second rod; add 21½" for header, casings, and fullness. Cut a piece of fabric the determined measurements, **piecing fabric panels** as necessary. Cut a length of eyelet trim 2" shorter than 1 long edge of fabric piece.

3. Make a 1" **double hem** along each short edge (side) of fabric piece. Make a 1" **single hem** along 1 long edge (top) of fabric piece; make a ½" **single hem** along bottom edge of fabric piece.

4. For header and casing at top of valance, **fuse** 1"w web tape along top edge on wrong side of fabric piece; **fuse** another length 1¼" below first length. Do not remove paper backing. Press edge of fabric 4¼" to wrong side. Unfold edge and remove paper backing. Refold edge and **fuse** in place.

5. For casing at bottom edge of valance, **fuse** ½"w web tape along bottom edge on wrong side of fabric piece; **fuse** another length 1¼" above first length. Do not remove paper backing. Press edge of fabric 2¼" to wrong side. Unfold edge and remove paper backing. Refold edge and **fuse** in place.

6. For eyelet trim, make a 1" **single hem** along each end of eyelet. **Fuse** ½"w web tape along bottom edge on wrong side of valance. Remove paper backing. With right side of eyelet facing wrong side of valance and straight edge of eyelet along top edge of web tape, **fuse** eyelet to valance.

7. Remove rods from window and insert through casings in valance; hang valance. Arrange pouf in valance, stuffing with tissue paper if desired to maintain shape.

DIAGRAM

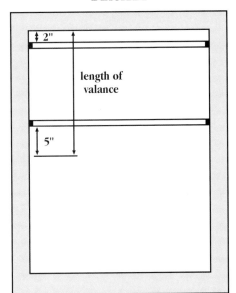

2"

length of valance

5"

*The projects on these pages require the use of the following techniques which are shown in **bold print** in the instructions. Please familiarize yourself with the General Instructions, pages 118 - 127, and these specific techniques before beginning the projects.*

- *Fusing (page 123)*
- *Piecing Fabric Panels (page 123)*
- *Making a Single Hem (page 124)*
- *Making a Double Hem (page 124)*

COVERED BENCH
(Shown on page 67)

You will need a bench with padded seat, fabric to cover seat, a cutwork table runner approx. 4" larger on all sides than seat, hot glue gun, glue sticks, and 2 yds of ⅞"w satin ribbon.

1. Remove seat from bench. Cut a piece of fabric large enough to wrap around padding of seat and overlap 2" onto bottom.

2. Center seat upside down on wrong side of fabric piece. Alternating sides and pulling fabric until smooth, glue edges of fabric to bottom of seat.

3. Replace seat on bench.

4. Center table runner on seat. Cut ribbon in half. Tie 1 ribbon length into a bow around each front corner of table runner; trim ends.

AMERICAN COUNTRY

*W*elcome home to the spirit of Early America! Homey touches that proclaim a genuine affection for our great land make this collection especially endearing. Red, white, and blue print fabrics set the tone for a Colonial ''keeping room.'' Draped across the table, quick-to-make patchwork runners serve as place mats, presenting a novel alternative to traditional table dressings. Made from fabrics reminiscent of Old Glory, chairback hearts and seat pads are tied to plain wooden chairs for an inviting look. The two homespun window treatments in this section are made with time-saving techniques. For this cozy scene, creamy tieback curtains trimmed with a starry blue print enhance the room's appeal. The curtain rod is concealed in a clever casing, and easy button-covered sashes hold the panels in place. Simple and simply charming, this nostalgic American decor celebrates two of our favorite things — home and country.

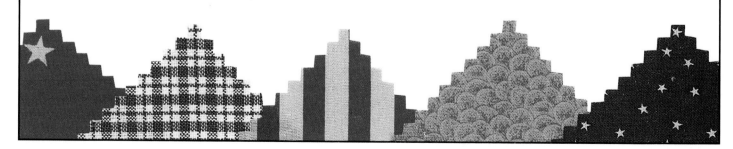

Tieback Curtains, page 91
Easy Trimmed Table Runner, page 89
Chair Pad, page 90

Tied Tab Curtains, page 89

82

Stars and stripes are forever inspiring new decorating ideas. Printed on fields of red, white, and blue fabric, the popular combination covers a trio of decorative boxes that serves as the base for a cheery lamp (left). Mixing homespun charm with practicality, our country baskets (below) are delightful accents for this cozy setting. Torn fabric strips add rustic appeal, and a wired-ribbon bow is amazingly simple — and a lot less expensive than the store-bought variety. The padded basket is much easier than it looks — the fabric is gathered using a rubber band!

Created with a modest blue-on-white striped material, these bow-tied tab curtains (opposite) are gentle reminders of simple country goodness and American pride. The decorative tabs and the star-studded border are a cinch to add.

Stacked Box Lamp, page 86
Country Baskets, page 86

A comfortable gathering place, the ''keeping room'' is unified with a decor of all-American prints, plaids, and stripes. The extra-easy decorative heart that's strung across the back of the chair (right) is an unmistakable expression of hospitality. And a fast-to-finish chair pad invites friends to sit a while and linger over good food and conversation. Because all the seams and appliqués are fused, our patriotic pillows (below) are a breeze to make. Buttons and jute are homey touches, and the ''stitching'' on the ''God Bless America'' pillow is actually done with a felt-tip pen!

A spectacular backdrop for our Americana collection, this patchwork wall hanging (opposite) offers a grand salute to the land that we love.

Heart Chair Decoration, page 91
Heart Patch Pillow, page 88
''God Bless America'' Pillow, page 88
Country Envelope Pillow, page 88

84

Spirited Wall Hanging, page 87

COUNTRY BASKETS

(Shown on page 83)

For padded basket, you will need a round basket, fabric to cover basket, polyester bonded batting, large rubber band, jute twine, masking tape, hot glue gun, and glue sticks.

For wire basket, you will need a wire basket with handle, fabrics to weave through basket, raffia, hot glue gun, and glue sticks.

For twig basket, you will need a twig basket with handle, muslin for liner, a red permanent felt-tip pen with fine point, instant coffee, a 3¹/₂" x 45" fabric strip for bow, ¹/₂"w paper-backed fusible web tape, 26-gauge florist wire, and wire cutters.

PADDED BASKET

1. Measure basket from 1 side of rim to opposite side of rim (**Fig. 1**); add 7". Cut a circle of fabric the determined measurement.

Fig. 1

2. For padding, measure height of basket; subtract 1". Measure around side of basket. Cut a strip of batting the determined measurements. With 1 long edge of batting along bottom edge of basket, glue batting around side of basket.

3. Center basket on wrong side of fabric circle. Bring edge of fabric to inside of basket and secure with tape. Place rubber band around fabric 1" below rim of basket. Remove tape and fold edge of fabric to wrong side, tucking edge under rubber band. If desired, use glue to secure fabric in place.

4. Wrap twine around basket, covering rubber band. Knot twine ends at front; trim ends. Form a multi-loop bow from twine; tie center of bow with twine to secure. Glue bow to knot at front of basket.

WIRE BASKET

1. Measure space between 2 wires in basket. Tear fabric strips the determined width.

2. Weave fabric strips through wire in basket as desired. Glue ends to secure.

3. Tie raffia into a bow; glue bow to basket handle.

TWIG BASKET

1. Tear a square of muslin for basket liner. **Coffee-dye** liner.

2. Use red pen and a ruler to draw dashed lines ¹/₂" from edge of liner to resemble stitches. Place liner in basket.

3. For bow, make **wired fabric ribbon** from fabric strip. Make a **wired ribbon bow** with 11" streamers from ribbon length. Wire bow to basket handle.

STACKED BOX LAMP

(Shown on page 83)

You will need a half-pint canning jar, a 3³/₄"l x 3³/₄"w x 4¹/₈"h box, a 7" dia. x 3"h box with lid, and a 9³/₈"l x 7³/₈"w x 5"h box with lid for lamp base; a jar lid lamp kit; fabrics to cover boxes and lids; a lampshade; fabric to cover lampshade; fabrics for trim on lampshade; paper-backed fusible web; ¹/₂"w paper-backed fusible web tape; tissue paper; removable tape; spray adhesive; fabric glue; aquarium gravel; hot glue gun; and glue sticks.

1. To cover boxes and lids, follow Covering Box portion of **Decorative Boxes**.

2. For trim on each lid, measure around side of lid; add 1". Use web tape and a 2¹/₈"w fabric strip to make ³/₄"w **fabric trim** the determined length. Press 1 end of trim ¹/₂" to wrong side. Beginning with unpressed end, use fabric glue to glue trim around side of lid.

3. For lamp base, hot glue lids onto boxes. Stack boxes from largest to smallest and hot glue boxes together.

4. Fill jar with gravel. Follow kit manufacturer's instructions to assemble lamp. Place lamp in top box.

5. Cover lampshade with fabric.

6. For trim along top edge of lampshade, measure around top edge of lampshade; add 1". Use web tape and a 2¹/₈"w fabric strip to make ³/₄"w bias **fabric trim** the determined measurement. Press 1 end of trim ¹/₂" to wrong side. Beginning with unpressed end of strip at lampshade seam, use fabric glue to glue trim along top edge of lampshade. Repeat for trim along bottom edge of lampshade.

7. Place lampshade on lamp.

SPIRITED WALL HANGING (Shown on page 85)

For an approx. 34¹/₂" x 42" wall hanging, you will need fabrics for wall hanging front and binding (see **Diagram** and **Table** for amounts), two 34¹/₂" x 42" pieces of muslin fabric for front and back of wall hanging, a 4" x 35" strip of fabric for hanging sleeve, a 34¹/₂" x 42" piece of fusible fleece, 36" of ¹/₂" dia. wooden dowel, two 2" dia. wooden beads with ¹/₂" dia. holes, four 2¹/₂"w wooden star cutouts, red and dark yellow acrylic paint, foam brushes, paper-backed fusible web, 1"w paper-backed fusible web tape, brown and black permanent felt-tip pens with fine points, hot glue gun, and glue sticks.

1. Fuse web to wrong sides of fabrics for A, B, C, D, E, F, and G pieces. Do not remove paper backing.

2. For wall hanging front and binding, refer to **Table** and cut pieces from fabrics. Remove paper backing.

3. (Note: Refer to **Diagram** for Step 3.) For wall hanging front, arrange A, B, C, D, and E pieces on right side of 1 muslin piece; **fuse** in place. Arrange F and G pieces 2³/₄" from edges of muslin piece; **fuse** in place. **Fuse** fleece to wrong side of wall hanging front.

4. Use brown pen and a ruler to draw dashed lines on muslin areas of front to resemble stitches.

5. Place front right side up over remaining muslin piece (back). Pin layers together.

6. For binding, make a 1" **single hem** along each end of top and bottom binding fabric strips. Make 1"w **binding** from all binding strips.

7. Insert 1 side edge of wall hanging into fold of 1 side binding strip; **fuse** in place. Repeat to apply remaining side binding strip to remaining side edge of wall hanging and top and bottom binding strips to top and bottom edges of wall hanging.

8. For hanging sleeve, press each end and then each long edge of fabric strip 1" to wrong side. **Fuse** web tape along each long edge on wrong side of fabric strip. Remove paper backing and **fuse** strip ¹/₂" from top edge on back of wall hanging.

9. Paint beads red and stars dark yellow. Use black pen to draw dashed lines along edges of stars to resemble stitches.

10. Insert dowel into hanging sleeve and hot glue beads to ends of dowel. Hot glue stars to wall hanging.

TABLE

FABRIC PIECE	SIZE	NUMBER NEEDED
A	34¹/₂" x 3¹/₂"	2
B	3¹/₂" x 42"	2
C	7¹/₂" x 5"	15
D	2¹/₂" x 2¹/₂"	8
E	4" x 2³/₄"	15
F	1" x 36¹/₂"	2
G	1" x 29"	2
side binding	4" x 42"	2
top & bottom binding	4" x 36¹/₂"	2

DIAGRAM

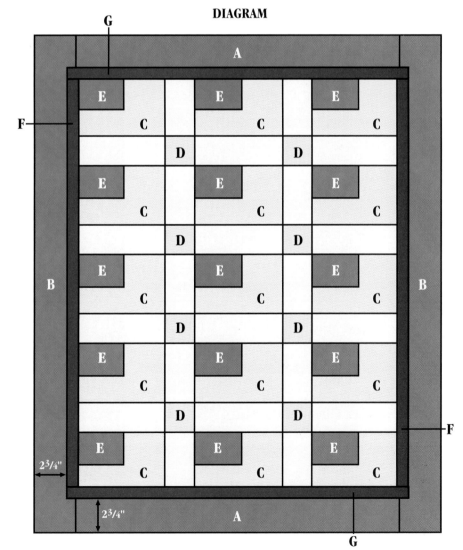

"God Bless America" Pillow (Shown on page 84)

For a 19" x 17½" pillow, you will need two 20½" x 19" fabric pieces for pillow front and back, one 11½" x 10½" piece of muslin for appliqué background, one 10" x 16" fabric piece for trim around muslin, one 5½" x 4" American flag for appliqué, two 9" lengths of jute twine, paper-backed fusible web, ¾"w paper-backed fusible web tape, black permanent felt-tip pen with fine point, instant coffee, ⅛" hole punch, disappearing ink fabric marking pen, and polyester fiberfill.

1. Coffee-dye muslin and flag.
2. Use hole punch to punch 1 hole ¼" from top left corner and another hole ¼" from bottom left corner of flag. Thread 1 length of jute twine through each hole and tie into a bow.
3. Fuse web to wrong sides of muslin and flag. Remove paper backing. **Fuse** muslin to center on right side of 1 pillow fabric piece (front). **Fuse** flag to center of muslin.
4. For trim around muslin, **fuse** web to wrong side of trim fabric piece. Cut two 1½" x 10½" strips and two 1½" x 13½" strips from fabric piece. Remove paper backing. Overlapping muslin ½", arrange 10½" trim strips along side edges of muslin and 13½" trim strips along top and bottom edges of muslin; **fuse** in place.
5. Use fabric marking pen and a ruler to draw horizontal lines ¼", 1", and 2" below top trim strip and ¼", 1¼", and 2" above bottom trim strip. Using lines as a guide, use fabric marking pen to write "God Bless America" on pillow front. Use fabric marking pen to draw lines ¼" from edges of flag. Using dashed lines to resemble stitches, use black pen to draw over letters and lines around flag.
6. Make **pillow** from pillow front and remaining fabric piece (back).

Country Envelope Pillow (Shown on page 84)

For a 16½" x 12½" pillow, you will need two 18" fabric squares for pillow front and back, two 17½" x 13½" pieces of muslin fabric for pillow form, polyester fiberfill, ¾"w paper-backed fusible web tape, five 1⅛" buttons, and fabric glue.

1. Fuse an 18" length of web tape 4" from 1 edge (top edge) on wrong side of pillow front fabric square. Do not remove paper backing.
2. Using pillow fabric squares, follow Steps 1 - 3 of **Making a Pillow**, leaving opening for turning along top edge of pillow.
3. For pillow form, use muslin pieces and make **pillow**.
4. Insert pillow form into pillow and position form at bottom of pillow.
5. For flap, remove paper backing from web tape inside pillow. **Fuse** pillow front and back together along web tape; **fuse** opening along edge of flap closed. Fold flap to front of pillow.
6. Spacing buttons approx. 2" apart, glue buttons across flap ½" above bottom edge of flap.

Heart Patch Pillow
(Shown on page 84)

For a 15" square pillow, you will need two 16½" fabric squares for pillow front and back, a 12" fabric square for appliqué background, fabrics for heart appliqués, 1⅝ yds of ⅜"w grosgrain ribbon, paper-backed fusible web, ⅜"w and ¾"w paper-backed fusible web tape, four ⅞" buttons, fabric glue, and polyester fiberfill.

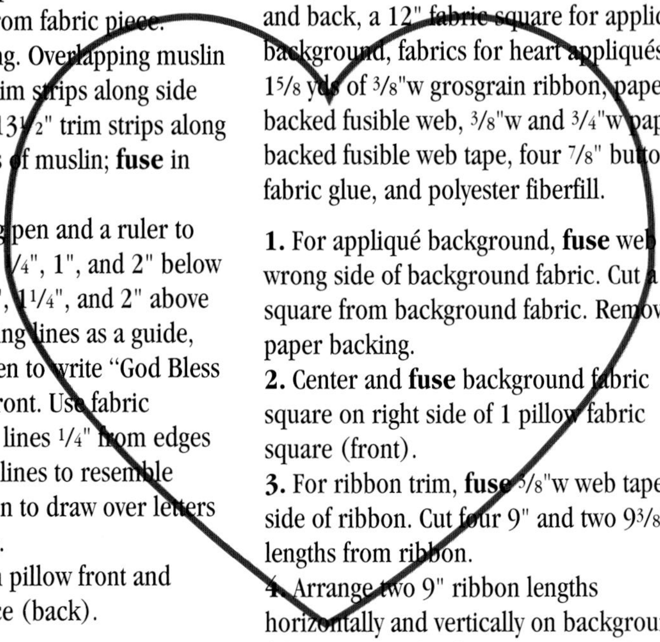

1. For appliqué background, **fuse** web to wrong side of background fabric. Cut a 9" square from background fabric. Remove paper backing.
2. Center and **fuse** background fabric square on right side of 1 pillow fabric square (front).
3. For ribbon trim, **fuse** ⅜"w web tape to 1 side of ribbon. Cut four 9" and two 9⅜" lengths from ribbon.
4. Arrange two 9" ribbon lengths horizontally and vertically on background fabric square, dividing square into 4 smaller squares; **fuse** in place. Center remaining 9" ribbon lengths over side edges of background fabric square and 9⅜" lengths over top and bottom edges of background fabric square; **fuse** in place.
5. For heart appliqués, trace heart pattern 4 times onto paper backing side of web. Cut hearts apart and **fuse** 1 traced heart to wrong side of each heart appliqué fabric. Cut out hearts. Remove paper backing.
6. Fuse hearts to background fabric square.
7. Using ¾"w web tape, make **pillow** from pillow front and remaining fabric square (back).
8. Glue 1 button to center of each heart appliqué.

TIED TAB CURTAINS (Shown on page 82)

You will need a spring-tension curtain rod, fabric for curtains, fabric for trim and tab ties, fabric for star appliqués, paper-backed fusible web, 1"w paper-backed fusible web tape, buttons, fabric glue, and spring-type clothespins.

1. Mount curtain rod.
2. To determine width of each fabric panel, measure length of rod; multiply measurement by 1¼. To determine length of each fabric panel, measure from top of rod to desired length; subtract 2½". Cut 2 fabric panels the determined measurements, **piecing fabric panels** as necessary.
3. (**Note:** Follow Steps 3 - 9 for each panel.) For fabric trim along bottom of panel, cut a 13"w fabric strip same length as bottom edge of panel. On right side of panel, **fuse** web tape along bottom edge; remove paper backing. With right sides facing, match 1 long edge (top) of trim strip to bottom edge of panel. **Fuse** trim to panel. Press seam allowance toward trim.
4. Make a 1" **single hem** along side edges of panel and trim.
5. Cut two 6" lengths of web tape. Referring to **Fig. 1**, **fuse** 1 length of web tape along each side edge on wrong side of trim; **fuse** web tape along bottom edge on wrong side of trim. Do not remove paper backing. Press bottom edge of trim 6" to wrong side. Unfold edge and remove paper backing. Refold edge and **fuse** in place.

Fig. 1

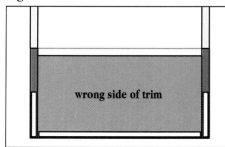
wrong side of trim

6. Make a 3" **double hem** along top edge of panel.
7. For star appliqués, trace desired number of stars onto paper backing side of web. Cut stars apart and **fuse** stars to wrong side of star appliqué fabric. Cut out stars. Remove paper backing. **Fuse** stars along trim on panel. Glue 1 button to center of each star.
8. To determine number of tab ties required for panel, measure width of panel and divide by 6; round up to the next whole number. Cut the determined number of 3⅝" x 36" fabric strips. Make 1¼"w **fabric trim** from each fabric strip. Matching ends, fold each trim length in half. Use a dot of glue to glue 3½" at folded end together; secure with clothespins until glue is dry.
9. Spacing tab ties evenly, position ties along top edge of panel with fold of each tie overlapping 3½" onto right side of panel (**Fig. 2**). Glue 3½" at folded end of each tie to panel; secure ties with clothespins until glue is dry.

Fig. 2

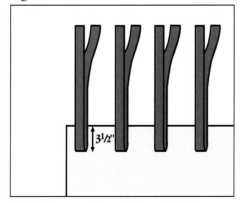

3½"

10. To hang each panel, tie tab ties into bows around curtain rod.

The projects on these pages require the use of the following techniques which are shown in **bold print** in the instructions. Please familiarize yourself with the General Instructions, pages 118 - 127, and these specific techniques before beginning the projects.

- *Coffee-dyeing (page 122)*
- *Fusing (page 123)*
- *Piecing Fabric Panels (page 123)*
- *Making a Single Hem (page 124)*
- *Making a Double Hem (page 124)*
- *Making Fabric Trim (page 125)*
- *Making a Pillow (page 127)*

EASY TRIMMED TABLE RUNNER
(Shown on page 81)

For each 20"w table runner, you will need fabric for table runner, 4 fabrics for trims, paper-backed fusible web, and ½"w paper-backed fusible web tape.

1. To determine length of table runner, measure width of table; add 25". Cut a 21"w fabric piece the determined length.
2. For trims along ends of runner, **fuse** web to wrong sides of trim fabrics. Do not remove paper backing. Cut two 6½" x 21" strips from 1 fabric, two 2" x 21" strips from second fabric, two 1¼" x 21" strips from third fabric, and two 1¼" x 21" strips from fourth fabric. Remove paper backing.
3. Fuse one 6½"w trim strip along each end of table runner. Overlapping long edges of strips as desired, **fuse** 1 trim strip from each remaining fabric along each end of table runner over 6½"w strips.
4. Make a ½" **single hem** along each edge of table runner.

CHAIR PAD

(Shown on page 81)

For each chair pad, you will need a chair, fabrics for pad top and backing, high-loft polyester bonded batting, extra-wide double-fold bias tape, paper-backed fusible web, 3/8"w paper-backed fusible web tape, craft paper or newspaper, fabric glue, and spring-type clothespins.

1. For chair pad pattern, measure chair seat to determine shape of pad (**Fig. 1**); use a pencil and ruler to draw shape on craft paper. Cut out pattern. Matching side edges, fold pattern in half and trim edges to make pattern symmetrical; unfold pattern.

Fig. 1

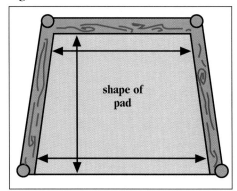

2. Fuse web to wrong sides of pad top and backing fabrics.

3. Use pattern to cut 1 shape each from top fabric, backing fabric, and batting. Trim 1/4" from all edges of batting shape.

4. Center batting on wrong side of backing fabric shape. Center top fabric shape right side up over batting. **Fuse** fabric pieces to batting; **fuse** fabric pieces together along edges.

5. For binding along front and side edges of pad, measure from back of pad along 1 side edge, along front of pad, and along remaining side edge; cut a length of bias tape the determined measurement.

6. Unfold center fold of binding. **Fuse** web tape along each long edge on wrong side of binding. Do not remove paper backing. Refold center fold of binding and press. Open binding and remove paper backing.

7. With 1 end of binding even with back edge of pad, insert 1 side edge of pad into fold of binding; **fuse** binding to side edge. Continue fusing binding to front and remaining side edge, mitering binding at corners. Use glue at corners of binding to secure miters; secure with clothespins until glue is dry.

8. For remaining binding and ties, measure back edge of pad; add 60". Cut a length of bias tape the determined measurement. Repeat Step 6 to apply web tape to binding. With back edge of pad centered in binding, insert back edge of pad into fold of binding and **fuse** binding to pad; **fuse** remainder of binding together to ends.

9. Place pad on chair. Loosely wrap ties around back of chair and tie into a bow at back; trim ends.

HEART PATTERN

HEART CHAIR DECORATION

(Shown on page 84)

You will need three 9" squares of fabric for heart (we used 3 different fabrics), one 9" square of poster board, paper-backed fusible web, 2 buttons, jute twine, hole punch, tracing paper, hot glue gun, and glue sticks.

1. **Fuse** web to wrong sides of fabric squares.
2. **Fuse** 1 fabric square to each side of poster board square.
3. Trace heart patterns, this page and page 90, onto tracing paper; cut out. Use large heart pattern to cut 1 heart from fabric-covered poster board. Use small heart pattern to cut 1 heart from remaining fabric square.
4. Center and **fuse** small heart to 1 side (front) of large heart.
5. Punch a hole ¼" from each side edge of heart. For hanging ties, loop center of 1 length of twine through each hole.
6. Glue 1 button close to each hole in heart.
7. Position heart as desired on chair back and loop ends of twine around uprights of chair back. Knot looped ends to form hanging loops; trim ends.

TIEBACK CURTAINS (Shown on page 81)

You will need a conventional curtain rod; fabric for curtains; contrasting fabric for side trim, casing, rod cover, and tiebacks; buttons; fabric glue; ¾"w paper-backed fusible web tape; and push pins.

1. Mount curtain rod.
2. To determine width of each fabric panel, measure length of curtain rod; multiply by 1½. To determine length of each fabric panel, measure from top of rod to desired length; add 13½". Cut 2 fabric panels the determined measurements, **piecing fabric panels** as necessary.
3. (**Note:** Follow Steps 3 - 5 for each panel.) Make a ¾" **single hem** along side edges of panel. Make a 2" **double hem** along 1 long edge (top) of panel. Make a 4" **double hem** along bottom edge of panel.
4. For trim along inside edge of panel, measure length of panel and subtract ½". Cut a fabric strip 4⅞"w by the determined measurement. Make a ¾" **single hem** along each end of strip. Make 2"w **fabric trim** from strip. **Fuse** web tape along each long edge on wrong side of trim. Remove paper backing. Beginning at bottom edge of panel, **fuse** trim 1½" from inside edge of panel.
5. For casing, measure width of panel; add 1½". Cut a fabric strip 4⅞"w by the

determined measurement. Make a ¾" **single hem** along each end of strip. Make 2"w **fabric trim** from strip. **Fuse** web tape along each long edge on wrong side of casing. Remove paper backing. **Fuse** casing 1½" from top edge of panel, covering top end of side trim.
6. With inside trim of each panel at center of rod, insert rod through casings. Hang curtains; pull curtains back to desired position.
7. For rod cover, measure length of area of rod to be covered; multiply by 3. Cut a fabric strip 4⅞"w by the determined measurement. Make a ¾" **single hem** along each end of strip. Make 2"w **fabric trim** from strip. Remove 1 panel from rod, insert rod cover onto rod, and replace panel on rod. Hang curtains.
8. For tiebacks, drape a tape measure around 1 panel in desired position; add 2" to measurement. Cut 2 fabric strips 6⅜"w by the determined measurement. Make a ¾" **single hem** along ends of each strip. Make 2¾"w **fabric trim** from each strip. Glue buttons to each tieback.
9. Drape tiebacks around panels, arranging pleats in panels as desired. Overlap ends of each tieback ½" and use push pins to secure to wall.

HEART PATTERN

CASUAL MIX

*S*ay hello to friendly, comfortable living! A playful combination of sunny yellow checks and polka dots, sky-blue gingham, and a rainbow of stripes and prints sets the mood for this easygoing ensemble. The lighthearted projects make it deliciously easy to awaken a sun room, morning room, or anyplace that needs a revival of color! Drape a welted skirt in eye-catching lemon yellow over a round table to create a relaxed dining area. Then, stripe it rich and whimsical with decorated wooden folding chairs! Strips of rickrack, ribbon, and fabric in a kaleidoscope of colors are glued along the sides and back of each chair, and the seats are padded with comfortable tie-on chair cushions. This very affordable collection offers two fresh window treatments to greet the sunshine. Framing the lively scene here, a simple swag is fashioned from a panel of blue gingham. The flowing drapes and poufs are easy to create with purchased window hardware. The awning-striped balloon shade shown on page 95 is a breeze to make with fusible ring tape. Our intriguing mix of casual and contemporary styles is guaranteed to let the fun shine in!

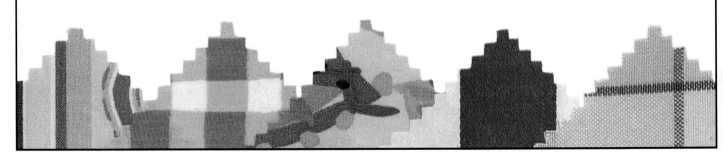

*S*imple accents placed here and there are deceptively easy ways to give your decor a unified look. Put together all of these splashy throw pillows (right) in a single afternoon! Spattered with white polka dots, a yellow knife-edge pillow is wrapped with a colorful fabric band. The blue striped pillow is tied with a ribbon bow, and rubber bands help give the round shirred pillow its gathers. A little spray paint and fabric borders turn clay flowerpots into pieces of modern art (below).

Beautiful and very affordable, the shirred balloon shade (opposite) in classic blue and white cabana stripes provides a crisp, clean look that's as fresh as all outdoors.

Pillowcase Pillow, page 98
Round Shirred Pillow, page 99
Knife-Edge Pillow with Fabric Band, page 98
Casual Flowerpots, page 99

Balloon Shade, page 102

Contemporary Covered Lamp, page 99
Picture Frames, page 101

*A*n outdated ottoman — a thrift shop find — is revived with a jazzy cover in a contemporary floral print (left). Decoupaged with plump blossoms, this versatile basket (below) is especially attractive filled with potted plants. The pretty bow topper is made of stiffened fabric strips.

Coordinating fabric, ribbons, and trim give an old lamp and lampshade (opposite) lighter, brighter appeal. Two fabric-covered photo frames take advantage of this collection's very mixable fabrics.

Covered Ottoman, page 100
Beribboned Basket, page 98

KNIFE-EDGE PILLOW WITH FABRIC BAND

(Shown on page 94)

You will need fabric for pillow, fabric for band, 3/4"w paper-backed fusible web tape, fabric glue, and polyester fiberfill.

1. For pillow, cut 2 fabric squares 1½" larger than desired finished size and make **pillow**.

2. For fabric band length, measure around pillow and add 1¼". For fabric band width, add 1½" to desired finished width. Cut a piece of fabric the determined measurements.

3. Make a ¾" **single hem** along each long edge and 1 short edge of fabric band. **Fuse** web tape along hemmed short edge on wrong side of band; remove paper backing. Overlapping remaining short edge ¾", **fuse** short edges together to form a tube.

4. With overlapped area at center back, slip fabric band around center of pillow. Use a dot of fabric glue to secure.

PILLOWCASE PILLOW (Shown on page 94)

You will need fabric for pillow, desired size pillow form, 3/4"w paper-backed fusible web tape, and 1 yd of grosgrain ribbon.

1. Measure length of pillow form and add 10"; multiply by 2. Measure width of pillow form; add 2". Cut a piece of fabric the determined measurements.

2. **Fuse** web tape along each long edge on right side of fabric piece. Do not remove paper backing. Matching right sides and short edges, press fabric piece in half.

Unfold fabric and remove paper backing. Refold fabric and **fuse** edges together.

3. Press raw edges at opening of pillowcase 4" to wrong side.

4. Turn pillowcase right side out and carefully push corners outward, making sure seam allowances lie flat; press.

5. Insert pillow form into pillowcase. To close pillowcase, tie ribbon into a bow around pillowcase.

BERIBBONED BASKET (Shown on page 97)

You will need a large basket, spray paint, print fabric for motifs on basket, fabric for bow, glossy Mod Podge® sealer, fabric stiffener, foam brushes, waxed paper, spring-type clothespins, matte clear acrylic spray, hot glue gun, and glue sticks.

1. Spray paint basket; allow to dry.

2. Cut desired motifs from print fabric. Apply Mod Podge® to wrong sides of motifs. Arrange motifs on basket. Use a warm, damp cloth to firmly press motifs in place and to remove excess Mod Podge®. Allow to dry.

3. Cut the following strips from bow fabric: 6" x 17", 6" x 25", 6" x 30", and 3" x 5".

4. Place 17", 25", and 30" long strips on waxed paper and use a clean foam brush to apply fabric stiffener to both sides of strips. Fold long edges of each strip 1½" to wrong side; use fingers to press smooth. Repeat for 5" long strip, folding long edges ¾" to wrong side. Use clothespins to hang strips on a clothes hanger; allow to dry for approx. 45 minutes.

5. With right side facing out, overlap ends of 17" long strip 1" to form a loop. Gather loop together at center and use a clothespin to hold in place. Repeat for 25" long strip.

6. To form bow, gather fabric at center of 30" long strip and use a clothespin to hold in place. Center larger loop, then smaller loop, on right side of 30" long strip. Pinch all 3 layers together at center and use clothespins to hold in place.

7. For bow center, apply fabric stiffener to wrong side of 5" long strip. Remove clothespins from bow and wrap strip around center of bow, overlapping ends at center back of bow. Use clothespins to hold strip in place.

8. Open loops of bow with fingers. Roll lengths of waxed paper and place inside loops to hold shape of loops. Allow bow to dry approx. 30 minutes (streamers should be slightly flexible at end of drying period). Remove waxed paper.

9. Position bow on basket handle. Hot glue bow to basket. Trim and notch ends of streamers. Allow bow to dry completely.

10. Spray basket and bow with acrylic spray.

Contemporary Covered Lamp (Shown on page 96)

You will need a lamp with shade, fabric to cover lamp, fabric to trim shade, polyester fiberfill, three 1 yd lengths of satin ribbon, fabric glue, 12" of ¼"w elastic, fabric marking pen, string, and thumbtack or pin.

1. To cover lamp base, refer to **Fig. 1** to measure lamp from 1 side of neck to opposite side of neck; add 10".

Fig. 1

2. Cut a fabric square 4" larger than the measurement determined in Step 1. Fold fabric square in half from top to bottom and again from left to right.

3. To mark cutting line, tie 1 end of string to fabric marking pen. Insert thumbtack through string at ½ the measurement determined in Step 1. Insert thumbtack through fabric as shown in **Fig. 2** and mark ¼ of a circle. Cut along drawn line through all layers of fabric. Unfold circle.

Fig. 2

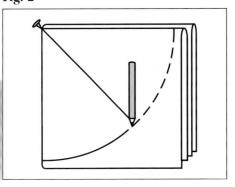

4. Center lamp on wrong side of fabric circle. Mark fabric where lamp cord extends from base of lamp. Cut a 1" long "X" in fabric at mark. Pull cord through "X" in fabric.

5. Bring edges of fabric up loosely around neck of lamp. Place fiberfill between lamp and fabric to achieve desired fullness. Gather fabric around neck and knot elastic securely around fabric and neck (**Fig. 3**). Fold edges of fabric to wrong side and tuck under elastic.

Fig. 3

6. Tie ribbon lengths together into a bow around fabric, covering elastic.

7. For trim along top edge of lampshade, measure around top edge of shade; add 1". Cut a 1"w bias fabric strip the determined measurement. Press each long edge and 1 short edge of fabric strip ¼" to wrong side. Beginning with unpressed end at seam of shade, glue strip along top edge of shade. Repeat for trim along bottom edge of shade.

Casual Flowerpots
(Shown on page 94)

For each pot, you will need a clay pot, spray paint, fabric, matte Mod Podge® sealer, foam brush, and paint pen(s) (optional).

1. Allowing to dry between coats, spray paint inside and outside of pot.

2. For fabric strip trim around pot, measure around rim of pot, add 1"; measure width of rim. Cut a strip of fabric the determined measurements. For fabric cutouts, cut out desired motifs from fabric. Apply sealer to wrong side of strip or motifs. Arrange strip or motifs on rim of pot. Firmly press in place. Allow to dry.

3. If desired, use paint pen(s) to decorate pot.

4. Allowing to dry between coats, apply 2 coats of sealer to rim of pot.

Round Shirred Pillow
(Shown on page 94)

For an approx. 15" dia. pillow, you will need a 50" square of fabric, 2 strong rubber bands, a 15" round pillow form, polyester fiberfill (optional), and fabric glue.

Follow Steps 1 - 4 of **Pillow with Stenciled Bow** to make pillow.

COVERED OTTOMAN (Shown on page 97)

You will need a round ottoman, fabric to cover ottoman, fabric for covered button and side trim, craft paper or newspaper, 2" thick foam rubber, electric knife, 1/4" thick foam core board, polyester bonded batting (optional), covered button kit (we used a 1⅞" button kit), large darning needle, heavy string, 1/4"w elastic, fabric marking pen, 1/2"w paper-backed fusible web tape, craft knife, 3" of hook and loop fastener tape, hook and loop fastener tape adhesive, thumbtack or pin, and safety pin.

1. For foam rubber pad pattern, place ottoman, top side down, on craft paper. Use a pencil to draw around top of ottoman; cut out pattern.
2. Place pattern on foam rubber and use fabric marking pen to draw around pattern. Use electric knife to cut out foam rubber along drawn line. Use pen to mark center of foam rubber circle.
3. To cover ottoman, place foam rubber circle on top of ottoman. Refer to **Fig. 1** to measure from bottom of 1 side of ottoman to bottom of opposite side; add 6".

Fig. 1

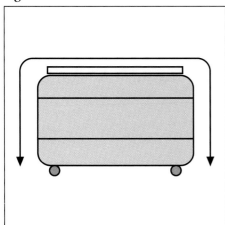

4. Cut a fabric square 4" larger than the measurement determined in Step 3, **piecing fabric panels** if necessary. Fold fabric square in half from top to bottom and again from left to right.
5. To mark cutting line, tie 1 end of string to fabric marking pen. Insert thumbtack through string at 1/2 the measurement determined in Step 3. Insert thumbtack through fabric as shown in **Fig. 2** and mark 1/4 of a circle. Cut along drawn line through all layers of fabric. Unfold circle. Mark center of circle with fabric marking pen.

Fig. 2

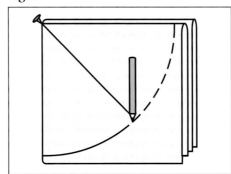

6. For casing, **fuse** web tape along edge on wrong side of fabric circle; do not remove paper backing. Press edge of fabric 1" to wrong side, easing excess fabric as necessary. Unfold edge and remove paper backing. Refold edge and **fuse** in place.
7. Cut a small slit on wrong side of casing. Attach safety pin to 1 end of elastic and thread elastic through casing. Pin ends of elastic together; pin to wrong side of casing.
8. Follow kit manufacturer's instructions to cover button with fabric.
9. Cut a square of foam board slightly smaller than foam rubber circle. Use craft knife to make 2 small holes 1" apart at center of foam board. Thread darning needle with a 24" length of string. Center foam rubber circle and fabric, right side up, on foam board square. Bring needle up

through 1 hole in foam board, through marked center of foam and fabric, and through button shank; bring needle back down through center of fabric and foam rubber and through remaining hole in foam board (**Fig. 3**). Pull string tight, creating an indentation in foam. Securely knot ends of string together and trim ends.

Fig. 3

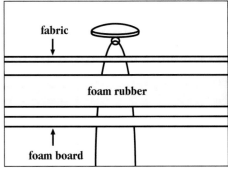

10. Place fabric cover on ottoman. If extra fullness is desired on top of ottoman, stuff batting between fabric and foam.
11. Unpin elastic and pull ends, gathering fabric tightly around bottom of ottoman. Trim excess elastic and pin ends back together again; tuck pinned ends into casing.
12. For side trim, measure around side of ottoman; add 6". Cut a 4"w strip of fabric the determined measurement. Make a 1/2" **single hem** along each long edge and 1 short edge of fabric strip.
13. Glue 1 side of hook and loop fastener tape along hemmed short edge on wrong side of fabric strip. Beginning with unpressed end, wrap fabric strip snugly around ottoman; mark placement for remaining side of tape on right side of strip. Glue remaining side of fastener tape in place. Wrap fabric strip around ottoman and secure with fastener tape.

PICTURE FRAMES (Shown on page 96)

For each frame, you will need a purchased precut mat for frame front (we used a 6" x 7" mat with a 3" x 4" opening and an 8" x 10" mat with a 4¹/₂" x 6¹/₂" opening), a piece of mat board same size as precut mat for frame back, a piece of mat board for frame stand (a 2" x 5" piece for small frame; a 2" x 7" piece for large frame), fabric, ribbon for trim (optional), removable fabric marking pen, spray adhesive, hot glue gun, and glue sticks.

1. To cover frame front, use fabric marking pen to draw around mat and mat opening on wrong side of fabric. Cutting 1" from drawn lines, cut out shape; at corners of opening in fabric, clip fabric to ¹/₈" from drawn lines (**Fig. 1**).

Fig. 1

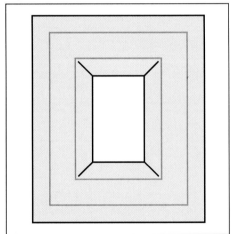

2. Apply spray adhesive to front of mat. Center mat, adhesive side down, on fabric and press in place. Fold fabric edges at opening of mat to back over edges of mat and hot glue in place. Fold corners of fabric diagonally over corners of mat and hot glue in place (**Fig. 2**). Fold remaining fabric edges to back of mat and hot glue in place.

Fig. 2

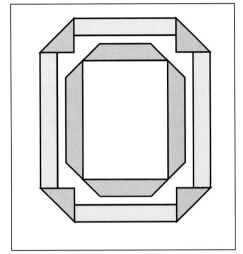

3. For optional ribbon trim, arrange ribbon lengths on frame front as desired. Fold ends of lengths to back of frame front and hot glue in place.

4. To cover frame back, measure width of mat board for frame back; add 2". Measure height of mat board; double measurement and add 2". Cut a piece of fabric the determined measurements.

5. Apply spray adhesive to 1 side of mat board. Place mat board, adhesive side down, on fabric piece and press in place (**Fig. 3**). Fold side edges of fabric to wrong side along side edges of mat board and hot glue in place. Fold bottom edge of fabric over mat board and hot glue in place. Fold top edge of fabric 1" to wrong side and hot glue in place. For back of frame back, fold top half of fabric over mat board and hot glue along edges to secure.

Fig. 3

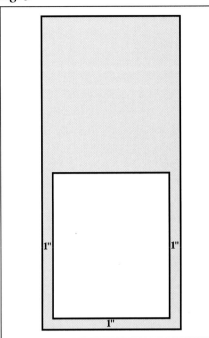

6. With right side of frame back facing wrong side of frame front, hot glue side and bottom edges of frame back to frame front, leaving opening at top for inserting photo.

7. To cover frame stand, repeat Steps 4 and 5. Fold top edge of frame stand 1¹/₂" to right side. With frame stand centered right side up on back of frame and bottom of frame stand even with bottom of frame, hot glue area of frame stand above fold to back of frame.

*The projects on these pages require the use of the following techniques which are shown in **bold print** in the instructions. Please familiarize yourself with the General Instructions, pages 118 - 127, and these specific techniques before beginning the projects.*

- *Fusing (page 123)*
- *Piecing Fabric Panels (page 123)*
- *Making a Single Hem (page 124)*

EASY WINDOW DECOR

(Shown on page 93)

The window treatment shown here uses one of the many types of hardware available today that reduce or eliminate the need for sewing, helping you create fast and easy decorative window treatments.

Some of the hardware is metal, while other types feature lightweight plastic. There are types of hardware, like the one shown, that help you create casual poufs and swags, and other types that give a more formal, pleated style. Many of these items use simple widths of fabric to create a decorator look. A trip to almost any fabric store will reveal a wealth of window treatment hardware choices to help you achieve the look you want.

The hardware we used is a plastic ring system made by EMSON® called Window Wonders™. We followed the manufacturer's instructions to mount the hardware and to drape and pouf lengths of fabric. For a more finished look, we used ¹/₂"w paper-backed fusible web tape to make **single hems** along the fabric edges before arranging the fabric in the rings.

BALLOON SHADE (Shown on page 95)

These instructions are for windows measuring up to 72" wide. Although the length of the shade is adjustable, the shade is designed to be stationary when hung.

You will need a ¹/₂" spring-tension rod, fabric for shade, 1"w paper-backed fusible web tape, ¹/₂"w fusible balloon shade tape, shade cord, scrap cardboard, and tissue paper (optional).

1. Mount rod in window 2" below top of window.

2. To determine width of each fabric panel for shade, measure length of curtain rod; multiply measurement by 2¹/₂ and divide by 3. To determine length of each panel, measure from top of rod to bottom of window frame; add 9" for header, casing, and hem. Cut 3 fabric panels the determined measurements, **piecing fabric panels** as necessary.

3. Follow Steps 3 and 4 of **Shirred Balloon Shade**.

4. To determine length of balloon shade tape, subtract 10¹/₂" from length of shade. With first ring of each tape length 1" from 1 end (bottom), cut 4 lengths of balloon shade tape the determined measurement.

5. Follow Steps 6 and 7 of **Shirred Balloon Shade**.

6. For header and casing, fuse 1"w web tape along top edge on wrong side of shade; fuse another length 1" below first length. Do not remove paper backing. Press top edge of shade 4" to wrong side. Unfold edge and remove paper backing. Refold edge and fuse in place.

7. Follow Steps 10 - 12 of **Shirred Balloon Shade** to complete shade.

WELTED ROUND TABLE SKIRT (Shown on page 93)

You will need a round table, fabric for skirt, ³/₄"w paper-backed fusible web tape, 1" dia. cotton cord, string, fabric marking pen, and thumbtack or pin.

1. Measure table for floor length skirt; add 8" for welting.

2. Cut a fabric square 4" larger than the measurement determined in Step 1, **piecing fabric panels** as necessary. Fold fabric square in half from top to bottom and again from left to right.

3. To mark cutting line, tie 1 end of string to fabric marking pen. Insert thumbtack through string at ¹/₂ the measurement determined in Step 1. Insert thumbtack through fabric as shown in **Fig. 1** and mark ¹/₄ of a circle. Cut along drawn line through all layers of fabric. Unfold circle.

Fig. 1

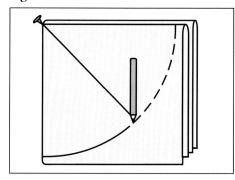

4. Fuse web tape along edge on wrong side of fabric circle; remove paper backing.

5. Place cord on wrong side of fabric circle approx. 3" from edge. Fold edge of fabric over cord and **fuse** edge to wrong side, easing excess fabric as necessary and trimming ends of cord to fit exactly. On right side of fabric, press along inner edge of cord.

DECORATED WOODEN CHAIRS (Shown on page 93)

For each chair, you will need a wooden folding chair, fabric for cushion and chair decoration, 2 yds of ⅝"w ribbon for cushion ties, ribbon and rickrack for chair decoration, 1" thick foam rubber, ½"w paper-backed fusible web tape, paper-backed fusible web, electric knife, and fabric glue.

CHAIR DECORATION

1. To decorate chair with fabric trim, measure width and length of area of chair to be covered; add 1" to each measurement. Cut a fabric strip the determined measurements. Make a ½" **single hem** along each edge of fabric strip. Glue fabric strip to chair.

2. To decorate chair with ribbon or rickrack, measure length of each area to be decorated. Cut a length of ribbon or rickrack the determined measurement. Glue length to chair.

CHAIR CUSHION

1. For cushion, measure length and width of chair seat. Use electric knife to cut a piece of foam rubber the determined measurements.

2. For cushion cover, measure length of foam rubber piece and double the measurement; add 8". Measure width of foam rubber piece; add 2". Cut a piece of fabric the determined measurements.

3. Make a ½" **single hem** along each short edge of fabric piece.

4. On right side of fabric piece, **fuse** web tape along each long edge; do not remove paper backing. Fold each short edge of fabric piece to right side, overlapping short edges 5" at center (**Fig. 1**); press. Unfold edges and remove paper backing. Refold edges and **fuse** in place.

Fig. 1

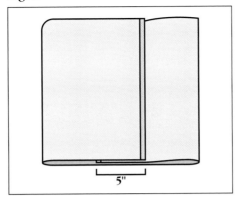

5. Cut two ⅞" squares from web. Cut each square in half diagonally.

6. At 1 corner of cover, match pressed line along 1 side edge to seam along adjoining edge and finger press corner flat (**Fig. 2**). Fuse 1 web triangle to bottom of corner (**Fig. 3**); do not remove paper backing. Press corner up along top edge of web triangle (**Fig. 4**). Unfold corner and remove paper backing. Refold corner and fuse in place. Repeat for remaining corners of cover.

Fig. 2

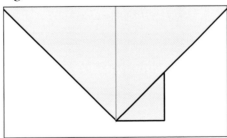

Fig. 3

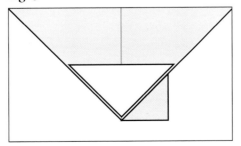

Fig. 4

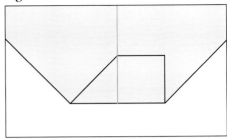

7. Turn 1 end of cover right side out; insert 1 end of foam rubber piece into cover. Carefully turn remaining end of cover right side out over foam rubber.

8. For ties, place cushion on chair seat. Cut two 1 yd lengths of ⅝"w ribbon. Fold each length in half. Glue fold of 1 ribbon length into small opening at each back corner of cushion (**Fig. 5**); allow to dry. Tie each tie into a bow around chair leg.

Fig. 5

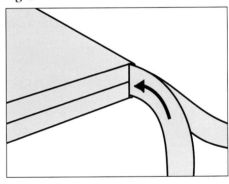

SPORTY RETREAT

*W*ithin the rich confines of this gentlemanly abode, an air of distinction prevails. Bold fabrics in striking checks, plaids, and paisleys are complemented by touches of gold and vintage accessories. Covered with comfortable, inexpensive flannel and piled with coordinating pillows, a favorite old chair is given new life. We used a finish-it-fast wraparound technique that allows you to complete your slipcover in a day! While a simple throw provides a warm accent for the room, a fun golf club lamp makes a bright conversation piece. The trio of window treatments in this section allows you to create an atmosphere that's custom-made to reflect his individual style. Here, tailored panels of checkered flannel are topped with a matching pleated valance (created with time-saving pleater tape) and sashed with dramatic black-on-red tiebacks. Encircling the room, a paisley fabric border brings masculine character to this sophisticated gentleman's retreat.

Gathered Draperies with Up-and-Down
Pleated Valance, page 116
Club Chair Slipcover, page 114
Fabric Wall Border, page 115
Golf Club Lamp, page 112

*T*he classic beauty of paisley print is always in style — especially in combinations of red and green. Here the richly toned fabric is matched with a complementing green and black plaid to create a simple stagecoach shade and valance (right). The shade is easily adjusted by rolling the fabric around a cardboard tube. Quick and easy to make, these fabric-covered boxes (below) provide additional storage space, as well as a decorator's touch. Best of all, they can be created from boxes of any size!

Stagecoach Shade with Padded Valance, page 11
Covered Storage Boxes, page 110

*T*he solitude of a gentleman's study makes it the ideal place for him to collect his thoughts or pen a letter to an old friend. A distinctive set such as this will keep correspondence essentials at his fingertips. As tasteful accents for a desk or writing table, the ensemble features a coordinating desk blotter, address book, pencil holder, and memo box, each of which began as a plain purchased item. Accentuated with gold trim, this easy fabric-covered collection is a rich addition to his retreat.

Desk Set, page 112

*E*xtra touches lend warmth and personality to a room. Simple props like these comfortable pillows and reversible throw (right) are invitations to relax and rejuvenate. Topped with a fabric-covered foam cushion, an antique valise inspired the suitcase footstool (below). Wooden finials make quick, sturdy legs.

Give him a new outlook with these floor-length draperies with a pinch-pleated valance (opposite). Made of a dashing red plaid, they punctuate the masculine theme. The customized valance is an extra-easy project because fusible pleater tape takes the guesswork out of measuring and gathering the pleats.

Pleated Draperies with Pinch-Pleated Valance, page 116

COVERED STORAGE BOXES

(Shown on page 106)

For each box, you will need an assembled cardboard storage box with lid, fabric(s) to cover box and lid, paper-backed fusible web, and fabric glue.

For box lid trim, you will **also** need 2 different widths of ribbon **or** 4 decorative brass corners with screws, hammer, nail, hot glue gun, and glue sticks.

1. To cover box lid, measure length and width of lid, including sides and ends (**Fig. 1**); add 3" to each measurement. Cut a fabric piece the determined measurements. **Fuse** web to wrong side of fabric piece. Do not remove paper backing.

Fig. 1

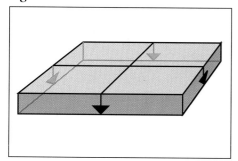

2. Center lid, top side down, on paper backing side of fabric piece. Use a pencil to draw around lid; remove lid. Draw lines 1" outside original drawn lines as shown in **Fig. 2**. Cut away corners of fabric piece and make a diagonal clip at each corner from outer drawn line to $1/16$" from original drawn line (**Fig. 3**). Remove paper backing.

Fig. 2

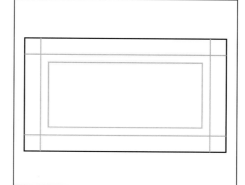

Fig. 3

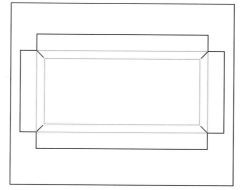

3. Center fabric piece, right side up, on top of lid. **Fuse** fabric to top of lid only. Turn lid over.

4. To cover each side of lid, **fuse** fabric to side of lid. Referring to **Fig. 4**, **fuse** ends of fabric covering side to ends of lid. Fold remaining edge of fabric to inside of lid; **fuse** in place. Use fabric glue to secure if necessary.

Fig. 4

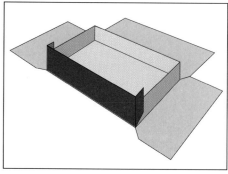

5. To cover each end of lid, fold short edges of fabric at 1 end of lid 1" to wrong side (**Fig. 5**); **fuse** in place. **Fuse** fabric to end of lid. Fold remaining edge of fabric to inside of lid; **fuse** in place. Use fabric glue to secure if necessary.

Fig. 5

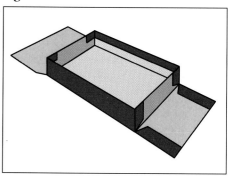

6. Repeat Steps 1 - 5 to cover box.

7. For ribbon trim on lid, measure around side of lid; add $1/2$". Cut 1 length of each width of ribbon the determined measurement. Center and use fabric glue to glue wide, then narrow, ribbon length around side of lid.

8. For decorative corners on lid, place 1 decorative corner on lid corner, use a pencil to mark placement of holes for screws, and remove corner. Use hammer and nail to make holes through lid at marks. Replace corner on lid; place screws through holes. Use hot glue to secure screws on inside of lid. Repeat for each remaining corner.

CREST PILLOW (Shown on page 108)

You will need two 19" x 12" fabric pieces; one $4^3/4$" felt circle; 2 yds of $1/2$" dia. cording with $1/2$" lip; 15" of $1/4$" dia. cording with $1/4$" lip; $1/2$"w paper-backed fusible web tape; white, silver, and gold dimensional fabric paint in squeeze bottles; a $4^1/4$" circle of lightweight cardboard; artist's tracing paper; dressmaker's tracing paper; fabric glue; and polyester fiberfill.

1. For appliqué, center cardboard circle on wrong side of felt circle on ironing board. At $1/2$" intervals, clip edge of felt to $1/8$" from cardboard. Press edges of felt over edge of cardboard. Remove cardboard and press felt circle again. Glue edge of felt in place.

2. Trace crest pattern onto artist's tracing paper. Use dressmaker's tracing paper to transfer pattern to center of felt circle. Referring to color key, paint design.

3. (**Note:** To prevent ends of cording from fraying after cutting, apply fabric glue to $1/2$" of cording around area to be cut, allow to dry, and then cut.) Glue lip of $1/4$" dia. cording along edge of appliqué, trimming ends to fit. Glue appliqué to center of 1 pillow fabric piece (front).

4. (**Note:** When making pillow, keep iron away from painted appliqué.) For pillow, **fuse** web tape along edges on right side of pillow front. Remove paper backing.

5. Beginning 2" from 1 end of $1/2$" dia. cording, **fuse** lip of cording to pillow front (**Fig. 1**), clipping lip at corners. Trim ends of cording to 1" from pillow front.

Fig. 1

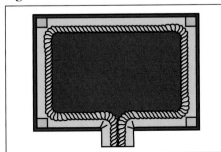

6. Fuse web tape to lip of cording along edge of pillow front except where free ends of cording meet. Remove paper backing.

7. Place pillow pieces right sides together. Leaving a 6" area open for turning and stuffing where ends of cording meet, **fuse** pillow back fabric piece to pillow front fabric piece.

8. Do not clip seam allowance at corners. Turn pillow right side out and carefully push corners outward, making sure seam allowances lie flat. Being careful not to fuse opening, press pillow. Stuff pillow with fiberfill. Cross ends of cording and tuck ends inside pillow (**Fig. 2**). **Fuse** edges of pillow together at opening. Where cording crosses, glue fabric and cording together as necessary.

Fig. 2

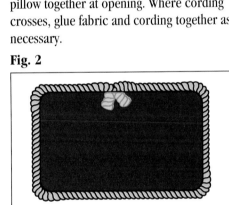

COLOR KEY

- ▢ white
- ▢ silver
- ▢ gold

KNIFE-EDGE PILLOWS
(Shown on page 108)

For each pillow, you will need fabric, $3/4$"w paper-backed fusible web tape, and polyester fiberfill.

Cut 2 fabric squares $1^1/2$" larger than desired finished size of pillow and make **pillow**.

EASY REVERSIBLE THROW
(Shown on page 108)

For a 48" x 60" throw, you will need a 48" x 60" fabric piece for front of throw and a 52" x 64" fabric piece for back of throw (see **Piecing Fabric Panels**) and $3/4$"w paper-backed fusible web tape.

1. On wrong side of 48" x 60" fabric piece, **fuse** web tape along each edge; remove paper backing.

2. Matching wrong sides, center 48" x 60" fabric piece on 52" x 64" fabric piece; **fuse** in place.

3. Make 1" **double hems** along edges of 52" x 64" fabric piece.

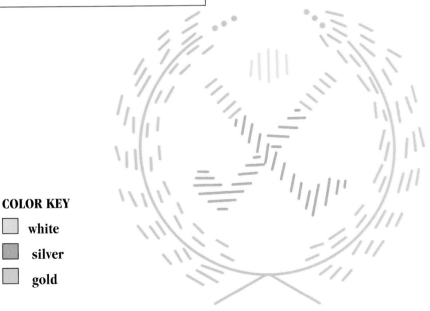

SUITCASE FOOTSTOOL (Shown on page 108)

This footstool is not designed for heavy wear or for supporting a person's full weight. Use as a footrest only.

You will need a suitcase (we found our 13³/₄"w x 24"l x 6¹/₂"d suitcase at an antique shop), 4 fence post finials for legs, hammer, nail, fabric for cushion, 2" thick foam rubber for cushion, electric knife, matte clear acrylic spray, 2"w webbed belting, safety pins, heavy-duty household cement, hot glue gun, glue sticks, and Design Master® glossy wood tone spray (optional; available at craft stores and florist shops).

1. If desired, spray finials with wood tone spray. Allow to dry.
2. Allowing to dry between coats, spray finials with 2 coats of acrylic spray.
3. Use a pencil to mark placement of each leg on 1 side (bottom) of suitcase. Use hammer and nail to "start" holes for finial screws at placement marks.
4. Apply household cement to bottom of each finial and screw into suitcase. Use cement on inside of suitcase to further secure screws.
5. For cushion, measure length and width of suitcase top. Use electric knife to cut 2 foam pieces slightly smaller than the determined measurements. Stack foam pieces together.
6. To cover foam pieces, measure around width of foam pieces (**Fig. 1**); add 2". Measure length of foam pieces; add 12". Cut a fabric piece the determined measurements.

Fig. 1

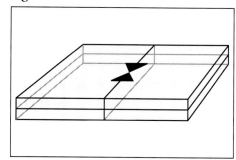

7. Wrap foam pieces "gift wrap" style with fabric piece, using safety pins to secure.
8. Place cushion on top of suitcase. Measure around width of suitcase and cushion together; add 4". Cut 2 lengths of belting the determined measurement.
9. Overlapping ends at bottom of suitcase, wrap lengths of belting snugly around suitcase and cushion; hot glue in place at bottom of suitcase.

GOLF CLUB LAMP (Shown on page 105)

You will need a floor lamp with shade, golf clubs, a golf ball, fabric to cover shade, fabric for bias trim on shade, ¹/₄"w ribbon, ³/₈"w paper-backed fusible web tape, spray paint (optional), tissue paper, spray adhesive, removable tape, hot glue gun, glue sticks, and fabric glue.

1. If desired, spray paint inside of lampshade.
2. Cover lampshade with fabric.
3. For trim along top edge of shade, measure around top of shade; add 1". Cut a 1¹/₂"w bias strip of fabric the determined measurement. Make ¹/₂"w **fabric trim** from fabric strip. Press 1 end of trim ¹/₂" to wrong side. Beginning with unpressed end at seam of shade, use fabric glue to glue trim along top edge of shade. Repeat for trim along bottom edge of shade.
4. Use ribbon to tie golf clubs to pole of lamp. Hot glue clubs to base of lamp to secure. Hot glue golf ball to top of lamp.

DESK SET (Shown on page 107)

For desk pad, you will need a desk pad, fabrics to cover side pads and center, ³/₈"w grosgrain ribbon, fabric glue, and spray adhesive.
For address book, you will need a 3-ring address book binder, fabric to cover binder, print fabric for appliqué on cover, fabric for appliqué background, ³/₈"w grosgrain ribbon, ¹/₈" dia. twisted cord, low-loft polyester bonded batting, paper-backed fusible web, lightweight cardboard, fabric glue, and spring-type clothespins.
For pencil holder, you will need a pencil holder with straight sides, spray paint (optional), fabric to cover holder, fabric for trim, ⁷/₈"w ribbon, ¹/₈" dia. twisted cord, and fabric glue.
For memo box, you will need a memo box with straight sides, spray paint (optional), fabric to cover sides and back of box, felt to cover front of box, fabric glue, and tracing paper.

DESK PAD

1. To cover side pads, measure length and width of 1 pad; add 2" to each measurement. Cut 2 fabric strips the determined measurements.
2. Press 1 long edge (inner edge) of each fabric strip 1" to wrong side.
3. Place 1 fabric strip right side up on 1 side pad, matching pressed edge of fabric to inner long edge of pad; use fabric glue to glue pressed edge in place. Allow to dry. Fold remaining edges of fabric strip to back of pad and use fabric glue to secure. Repeat for remaining side pad.
4. To cover center, measure width of exposed center and add 2". Measure length of exposed center. Cut a fabric piece the determined measurements. Cut 2 lengths of ribbon same length as width of fabric piece. Use spray adhesive to glue fabric to center, tucking short edges under side pads. Use

fabric glue to glue ribbon lengths along top and bottom edges of center, tucking ends under side pads.

ADDRESS BOOK

1. Open binder and lay flat. Measure length of binder from top to bottom. Cut two $2^1/2$"w fabric strips the determined measurement. Center and glue 1 fabric strip to binding with 1 long edge of strip placed $1/4$" under 1 long edge of binder hardware. Repeat with remaining fabric strip.

2. To cover outside of binder, measure length and width of open binder. Cut a piece of batting the determined measurements. Cut a fabric piece 1" larger on all sides than batting.

3. (**Note:** For Steps 3 - 7, secure fabric with clothespins until glue is dry.) With binder closed, glue batting to outside of binder.

4. Center open binder on wrong side of fabric piece. Fold corners of fabric diagonally over corners of binder; glue in place. Fold short edges of fabric over side edges of binder; glue in place. Fold long edges of fabric over top and bottom edge of binder, trimming fabric if necessary to fit around binder hardware; glue in place.

5. To cover inside of binder, cut 2 pieces of cardboard $1/2$" smaller on all sides than front of binder. Cut 2 fabric pieces 1" larger on all sides than 1 cardboard piece.

6. Center 1 cardboard piece on wrong side of 1 fabric piece. Fold edges of fabric over edges of cardboard; glue in place. Repeat for remaining cardboard piece.

7. Center and glue covered cardboard pieces to inside covers of binder.

8. For front of binder, **fuse** web to wrong sides of appliqué and background fabric pieces.

9. For appliqué, cut an oval from print fabric with desired motif at center. Cut a

rectangle from background fabric at least 1" larger on all sides than oval. **Fuse** background fabric piece, then appliqué, to center front of binder.

10. For ribbon trim, measure width and length of background; add 1" to each measurement. Cut 2 lengths of ribbon the determined width measurement and 2 lengths the determined length measurement. Arrange ribbon lengths over raw edges of appliqué background; trim overlapping ribbon ends at a 45 degree angle to form mitered corners. Glue ribbon lengths in place.

11. (**Note:** To prevent ends of cord from fraying after cutting, apply fabric glue to $1/2$" of cord around area to be cut, allow to dry, and then cut.) Beginning at center bottom, glue cord along raw edge of appliqué, trimming cord to fit exactly.

12. Cut an 8" length of cord. Tie a loose double knot at center of cord. Knot each end of cord and fray ends. Glue double knot to bottom center of appliqué.

PENCIL HOLDER

1. If desired, spray paint pencil holder.

2. Measure height of pencil holder and add 1"; measure around holder and add 1". Cut a fabric piece the determined measurements. For trim, cut a length of ribbon and a 1"w fabric strip same length as fabric piece.

3. Press long edges and 1 short edge of holder fabric piece $1/2$" to wrong side. Beginning with unpressed edge, glue fabric around pencil holder.

4. For trim, press long edges and 1 short edge of trim fabric strip $1/4$" to wrong side. Glue ribbon around holder $1/2$" from top edge. Beginning with unpressed edge, glue fabric strip along center of ribbon.

5. Cut an 8" length of cord. Tie a loose double knot at center of cord. Knot each end of cord and fray ends. Glue double knot to center of trim on holder.

MEMO BOX

1. If desired, spray paint memo box.

2. To cover sides and back of box, measure height of box; add 1". Measure sides and back of box from 1 front edge around back to remaining front edge; add 1". Cut a fabric strip the determined measurements.

3. Press long edges of fabric strip $1/2$" to wrong side.

4. Beginning $1/2$" from 1 end of strip, glue fabric strip around sides and back of box. Glue ends of strip to front of box.

5. To cover front of box, place box, front side down, on tracing paper; draw around box front. Cut out pattern. Use pattern to cut a piece of felt. Glue felt to front of box.

*The projects on these pages require the use of the following techniques which are shown in **bold print** in the instructions. Please familiarize yourself with the General Instructions, pages 118 - 127, and these specific techniques before beginning the projects.*

- *Fusing (page 123)*
- *Making Fabric Trim (page 125)*
- *Covering Lampshade with Fabric (page 127)*

These instructions are for covering a chair with loose seat and back cushions.

You will need a club chair, fabric (the slipcover for our 29"w x 32"h x 37"d chair required approx. 9 yds of 60"w flannel fabric), 1"w paper-backed fusible web tape, large safety pins, eight 3" long kilt pins (available at fabric stores), 1"w elastic, and strong rubber bands.

1. Remove cushions from chair.

2. To determine length of fabric piece to cover back, arms, and seat of chair, measure chair from center of back bottom edge to top of chair, from top to seat, to front of seat, and down to front bottom edge (**Fig. 1**); add 6". To determine width of fabric piece, measure chair at widest point from 1 side bottom edge to top of arm, down to seat, across seat, to top of remaining arm, and down to remaining side bottom edge (**Fig. 2**); add 6". Cut a fabric piece the determined measurements. If **piecing fabric panels** is necessary, position seam so it will fall between 1 arm and seat of chair.

Fig. 1

Fig. 2

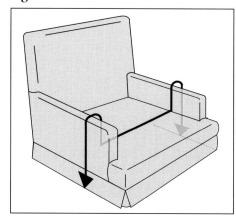

3. (**Note:** For remaining steps, use safety pins to pin fabric in place unless otherwise indicated.) Center fabric piece over chair. Tuck fabric between arms and chair back and between arms and seat, smoothing fabric over chair. Use pins to secure fabric in areas where pins will be concealed by cushions.

4. At back of chair, lift center back edge of fabric and smooth excess fabric from sides toward center of chair back. Use pins to secure excess fabric to back of chair, concealing pins under overlapping fabric (**Fig. 3**). Adjust overlapping fabric so that folds meet side edges of chair. Use kilt pins to pin fabric in place (see **photo**, page 115).

Fig. 3

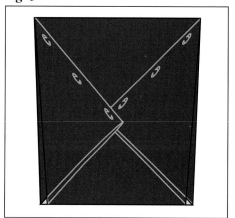

5. At front edge of each side of chair, roll remaining excess fabric from front toward back until cover fits snugly around bottom of chair (**Fig. 4**). Use 1 kilt pin at each front edge to secure excess fabric. Trim fabric that extends beyond bottom edge of chair even with bottom of chair.

Fig. 4

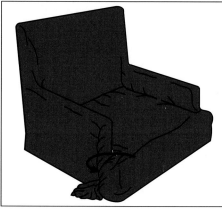

6. Use pins to secure bottom edge of cover to chair.

7. For skirt, determine desired placement for top edge of skirt. Measure around chair at this level; add 4". Determine desired length of skirt; multiply by 2 and add 1⅛". Cut a piece of fabric the determined measurements, **piecing fabric panels** as necessary. Cut a length of elastic 12" longer than length of fabric piece.

8. To make skirt, make **fabric trim** from fabric piece.

9. Insert elastic through skirt, centering elastic inside top edge (**Fig. 5**).

Fig. 5

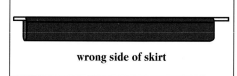

wrong side of skirt

10. With wrong side of skirt facing chair, refer to **Fig. 6** and pin left end of skirt to back of chair, beginning 2" from back right corner of chair; pin end of elastic to chair.

Fig. 6

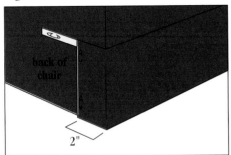

11. Pulling elastic taut, wrap skirt around chair, covering bottom edge of slipcover. Concealing pins behind skirt, pin skirt in place at each remaining corner of chair.

12. Approx. 4" from remaining end of skirt, cut a 1" opening near top edge on wrong side of skirt; thread elastic through opening and pin elastic to back of chair approx. 1" from back right corner (**Fig. 7**). Trim excess elastic. Fold remaining end of skirt to wrong side even with corner of chair and pin in place at top and bottom.

Fig. 7

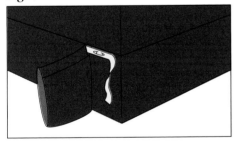

13. To determine size of fabric piece needed to cover each cushion, measure around width of cushion; add 6". Measure length of cushion; multiply by 2¹/₂. Cut a fabric piece the determined measurements, **piecing fabric panels** as necessary.

14. To cover seat cushion, center cushion, top side down, on wrong side of fabric

piece. Fold 1 raw edge of fabric to bottom of cushion; pin in place (**Fig. 8**). Press opposite raw edge of fabric 1" to wrong side. Wrap fabric around cushion, overlapping pressed edge over pinned edge; pin pressed edge in place. Fold remaining edges of fabric to center bottom of cushion and wrap with a rubber band to secure (**Fig. 9**). Repeat for back cushion. Place cushions in chair.

Fig. 8

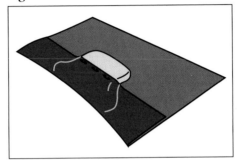

Fig. 9

The projects on these pages require the use of the following techniques which are shown in **bold print** in the instructions. Please familiarize yourself with the General Instructions, pages 118 - 127, and these specific techniques before beginning the projects.

- *Fusing (page 123)*
- *Piecing Fabric Panels (page 123)*
- *Making Fabric Trim (page 125)*

FABRIC WALL BORDER

(Shown on page 105)

You will need fabric, ³/₈"w and ⁵/₈"w ribbon for trim, ³/₈"w paper-backed fusible web tape, wallpaper paste, and wallpaper paste brush and smoothing brush (available at paint and wallpaper stores).

1. For border, cut fabric piece(s) the desired width and length to fit wall(s), **piecing fabric panels** as necessary.

2. For trim, cut 2 lengths of each width of ribbon same length as fabric piece(s). **Fuse** web tape along wrong side of each ribbon length. Remove paper backing from ³/₈"w ribbon lengths only.

3. Fuse ³/₈"w ribbon lengths along center of ⁵/₈"w ribbon lengths. Remove paper backing from ⁵/₈"w ribbon lengths. **Fuse** ribbon lengths along each long edge of fabric piece(s).

4. On a covered work surface, use paste brush to apply a thin coat of paste to wrong side of border. While paste is still wet, apply border to wall, smoothing border with smoothing brush.

GATHERED DRAPERIES WITH UP-AND-DOWN PLEATED VALANCE (Shown on page 105)

You will need 1 double conventional curtain rod set, fabric for drapery panels and valance, 3½"w fusible up-and-down pleat 4-cord shirring tape, 2½" drapery hook pins, 1½"w and 2"w grosgrain ribbon, 2 clear push pins, 1"w and 1½"w paper-backed fusible web tape, and scrap cardboard.

DRAPERIES

1. Mount curtain rod set.

2. For draperies, follow Steps 2 - 5 of Draperies portion of **Draperies with Swag Valance**.

3. For tiebacks, drape a tape measure around 1 drapery panel in desired position; add 2". Cut 2 lengths from each width of ribbon the determined measurement. Use 1½"w web tape to **fuse** one 1½"w ribbon length to center of each 2"w ribbon length.

4. For each panel, drape 1 tieback around panel and overlap ends 2"; insert push pin through overlapped area into wall behind draperies.

VALANCE

1. Determine finished valance width by measuring length of valance rod from end to end (**Fig. 1**).

Fig. 1

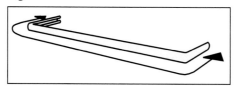

2. For width of valance fabric, multiply finished valance width (Step 1) by 2½. For length of valance fabric, measure from top of mounted valance rod to desired finished length; add 8¾" for header and hem. Cut a fabric piece the determined measurements, **piecing fabric panels** as necessary.

3. Use 1"w web tape to make a 1" **single hem** along 1 long edge (top) of fabric piece. Use 1"w web tape to make a 1" **double hem** along each side edge and a 3" **double hem** along bottom edge of fabric piece.

4. For pleats, cut a length of shirring tape 1" shorter than width of hemmed fabric piece. Beginning ½" from 1 side edge, **fuse** shirring tape ½" below top edge on wrong side of fabric piece.

5. Pull cords of shirring tape to gather fabric piece to finished valance width (Step 1). Securely knot cords; wrap excess around a small piece of cardboard and pin to back of valance.

6. Spacing hooks pins approx. 1½" apart, insert hook pins into shirring tape (**Fig. 2**). Hang hooks over valance rod.

Fig. 2

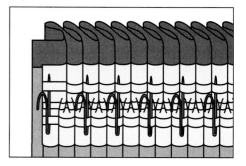

PLEATED DRAPERIES WITH PINCH-PLEATED VALANCE (Shown on page 109)

You will need 1 double conventional curtain rod set, fabric for drapery panels and valance, 1⅛" dia. clip-on café curtain rings, 3"w pinch pleat shirring tape, 2½" drapery hook pins, 1"w paper-backed fusible web tape, scrap cardboard, and 6"w strips of scrap fabric for "dressing" draperies (optional).

DRAPERIES

1. Mount curtain rod set.

2. For draperies, follow Steps 2 - 5 of Curtains portion of **Café Curtains with Lined Valance**.

VALANCE

1. Determine finished valance width by measuring length of valance rod from end to end (see **Fig. 1**, this page). For width of valance fabric, multiply finished valance width by 2½. For length of valance fabric, measure from top of valance rod to desired finished length; add 6" for header and hem. Cut a fabric piece the determined measurements, **piecing fabric panels** as necessary.

2. Make a 1" **single hem** along 1 long edge (top) of fabric piece, a 1" **double hem** along each short edge of fabric piece, and a 2" **double hem** along bottom edge of fabric piece.

3. For pleats, cut a length of shirring tape 1" shorter than width of hemmed fabric piece; **fuse** web tape along each long edge on wrong side of shirring tape. Remove paper backing. Beginning ½" from 1 side edge, **fuse** shirring tape ⅛" below top edge on wrong side of fabric piece.

4. Pull cords of shirring tape to gather fabric piece to finished valance width (Step 1). Securely knot cords; wrap excess around a small piece of cardboard and pin to back of valance.

5. Press pleats across width of valance. If desired, have a professional dry cleaner set the pleats.

6. Insert 1 hook pin into shirring tape at each pleat. Hang hooks over valance rod.

You will need a ¹/₂" dia. spring-tension curtain rod for shade; 2 conventional curtain rods for valance; fabrics for shade, shade lining, valance, and valance trim; ¹/₂"w paper-backed fusible web tape; a 2" dia. cardboard tube (we used a tube from a roll of gift wrap); 1¹/₂"w ribbon; and fusible fleece.

SHADE

1. Mount tension rod in top of window. Use a pencil to mark placement of rod in window.

2. To determine width of shade fabric piece, measure length of mounted rod; add ¹/₂". To determine length of shade fabric piece, measure from top of rod to windowsill; add 11". Cut 1 shade fabric piece and 1 lining fabric piece the determined measurements, **piecing fabric panels** as necessary.

3. On right side of shade fabric piece, **fuse** web tape along top and bottom edges. Beginning 2" from top edge of fabric, **fuse** web tape along each side edge (**Fig. 1**). Remove paper backing.

Fig. 1

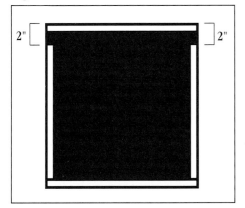

4. Using shade fabric and lining fabric pieces, follow Steps 2, 3, and 5 of **Making a Pillow**.

5. Insert rod through openings at top of side edges of shade. Hang shade.

6. To roll shade, cut 2 ribbon lengths twice the length of shade. Hang ribbons over top of shade. Roll bottom of shade toward front onto cardboard tube. Secure shade by tying ends of ribbons into bows at bottom.

VALANCE

1. Mount curtain rods with bottom rod positioned at desired finished length of valance.

2. To determine width of fleece for padding, measure length of 1 curtain rod from end to end (see **Fig. 1**, page 116). To determine length of fleece, measure from top of first rod to bottom of second rod. Cut a piece of fleece the determined measurements.

3. To determine width of valance fabric piece, add 1" to width of fleece piece. To determine length of valance fabric piece, double length of fleece piece and add 2¹/₂". Cut a fabric piece the determined measurements, **piecing fabric panels** as necessary.

4. On wrong side of fabric piece, center and **fuse** fleece with 1 long edge of fleece 2" from 1 long edge (top) of fabric piece.

5. Make a ¹/₂" **single hem** along side edges, then top edge, of fabric piece.

6. On wrong side of fabric piece, **fuse** web tape along top and bottom edges, 1¹/₂" below bottom edge of fleece, and along side edges between bottom 2 lengths (**Fig. 2**). Do not remove paper backing.

Fig. 2

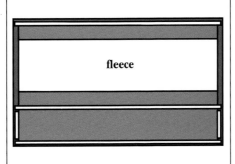

fleece

7. Press bottom edge of fabric piece to wrong side even with top edge of fleece. Press top edge of fabric to wrong side along top edge of fleece. Unfold fabric edges and remove paper backing. Refold fabric edges and **fuse** in place.

8. For trim on valance, measure width of finished valance; subtract 4". Cut 1 fabric strip 5⁵/₈"w by the determined length. Measure length of finished valance. Cut 2 fabric strips 5⁵/₈"w by the determined measurement. Make 2¹/₂"w **fabric trim** from each fabric strip.

9. Make a ¹/₂" **single hem** along ends of short fabric trim strips. **Fuse** ¹/₂"w web tape along all edges on wrong sides of all fabric trim strips. Remove paper backing.

10. Center long trim strip 1" from bottom edge on right side of valance. With 1 end even with top edge of valance, place short trim strips 1" from each side edge of valance. **Fuse** trim strips in place.

11. Insert rods through openings at side edges of valance. Hang valance.

---

*The projects on these pages require the use of the following techniques and additional project instructions which are shown in **bold print** in the instructions. Please familiarize yourself with the General Instructions, pages 118 - 127, and these specific techniques and instructions before beginning the projects.*

- *Fusing (page 123)*
- *Piecing Fabric Panels (page 123)*
- *Making a Single Hem (page 124)*
- *Making a Double Hem (page 124)*
- *Making Fabric Trim (page 125)*
- *Making a Pillow (page 127)*
- *Draperies with Swag Valance (page 20)*
- *Café Curtains with Lined Valance (page 60)*

GLOSSARY

This glossary includes a brief explanation of some of the products and techniques used in this book and is not meant to be a complete listing.

FUSIBLE PRODUCTS AND TECHNIQUES

• **fuse** – to join 2 surfaces by melting the adhesive in a fusible product with an iron (see Fusing, page 123).

• **fusible** – iron-on; any product that includes an adhesive that is activated by heating with an iron.

• **paper-backed fusible web (A)** – a fusible adhesive with a protective paper or silicone backing that is sold by the yard. Web is fused, paper backing side up, to 1 surface, paper backing is removed, and then web is fused to another surface, joining the 2 surfaces. Brands include: Pellon® Wonder Under®, Dritz® Magic Fuse™, and Therm O Web HeatnBond™.

• **paper-backed fusible web tape (B)** – paper-backed fusible web in precut widths on rolls; used for seams, hems, and to fuse trims to projects. Brands include: Conso® Thermo-Fuse™ Hem-N-Trim, Pellon® Wonder Under®, Dritz® Iron-On Hem-n-Trim™, and Therm O Web HeatnBond™.

• **fusible fleece (C)** – a thin, dense batting with fusible adhesive on 1 side; used for padding.

• **balloon shade tape (D)** – ring tape that creates soft drapes when gathered using a fine cord; used in Shirred Balloon Shade, page 78, and Balloon Shade, page 102.

• **decorative shirring tapes (E - H)** – tapes that consist of a single cord or several cords inside a fabric tape casing. The tapes are fused to fabric, and when cords are pulled, the tapes create shirring or pleats in the fabric. (**Helpful hint:** Use tweezers to pull ends of cord out of tape.) Some

shirring tapes are available in fusible form. Those that are not can be fused using paper-backed fusible web tape (see Fusing, page 123). Brands include: Conso®, Gosling®, and Dritz®. We used the following types of shirring tape in this book:

  single-cord shirring tape (E) – creates a single row of soft gathers; used in Tissue Box Cover, page 73.

  double-cord shirring tape (F) – creates narrow shirring; used in Covered Wastebasket, page 73.

  pinch pleat shirring tape (G) – creates pinch pleats; used in Pinch-Pleated Valance, page 116.

  up-and-down pleat shirring tape (H) – creates up-and-down pleats; used in Up-And-Down Pleated Valance, page 116.

OTHER ADHESIVES

• **fabric glue** – non-water soluble, washable glue specifically made for fabric. Brands include: Aleene's™ OK TO WASH IT™ and Beacon FABRI TAC.

• **hot glue** – comes in the form of sticks that are melted in an electric glue gun; provides a strong, long-lasting bond in items that will not be washed or dry cleaned.

OTHER PRODUCTS

• **liquid fray preventative** – used on raw edges of fabric to prevent raveling.

• **polyester bonded batting** – polyester fibers bonded into a layer of even thickness; used for padding.

• **polyester fiberfill** – loose polyester fibers; used to stuff pillows.

DRAPERY HARDWARE

• **conventional rod (I)** – ³/₄"w standard metal or clear plastic rod.

• **double conventional rod (J)** – 2 conventional rods mounted on the same brackets; used to hang 2 layers of window treatments together.

• **Continental® rod (K)** – 2¹/₂"w or 4¹/₄"w conventional rod used to add emphasis to top of window treatment; used in Draperies with Swag Valance, page 20.

• **decorative pole rod (L)** – 1¹/₄" dia. rod made to be seen; decorative brackets and finials may be used.

• **spring-tension rod (M)** – ¹/₂" dia. rod fits inside window frame and requires no brackets.

• **sash rod** – ¹/₂" rod with short returns used on doors.

• **drapery hook pin (N)** – a pin with a hook at 1 end; inserted into drapery shirring tape along a drapery or valance header, they are used to hang window treatments made with shirring tapes.

• **clip-on café ring (O)** – 1¹/₈" dia. metal rings for hanging curtains which do not have a casing; used in Café Curtains, page 60, and Pleated Draperies, page 116.

FABRIC TERMS

• **design repeat** – the distance from beginning to end of a design in a printed fabric; sometimes the repeat is indicated on the selvage of a fabric by repeat marks (+).

• **fullness ratio** – the number used to multiply by to determine the finished width of a fabric piece for fullness when gathering or pleating (we used 2¹/₂ for most of the projects in this book); for lighter or heavier weight fabrics, the fullness ratio may be raised to 3 or more or lowered to 2 or less, except where shirring tapes limit to an exact fullness ratio.

• **railroading** – using the width of fabric for the length of panels in a project; requires less piecing of fabric panels.

GENERAL INSTRUCTIONS

INTRODUCTION

So many fusible products and fabric adhesives are available now that it is possible to create both casual and elegant decorative accessory items, slipcovers, and window treatments without sewing a stitch!

The projects in this book are assembled using paper-backed fusible web, paper-backed fusible web tape, and fusible decorator notions. Fabric glue and hot glue are also used to add trims or for extra holding power at stress points.

Although the techniques used in constructing these projects are similar to those used in sewing, there are many differences as well. For this reason, whether you sew or not, we recommend that you familiarize yourself with both the instructions for your chosen project and these General Instructions before beginning your project.

ESTIMATING SUPPLIES

Specific amounts are not listed for some supplies in the projects. Read through all of the instructions for your project before measuring for and purchasing supplies. Take any measurements as described in project instructions, then check your measurements. For many projects, measuring is the single most important step toward successful results.

You may wish to purchase 10 to 20 percent extra of the fabrics and trims you will need for "insurance" against flaws, errors, etc. Coordinating pillows, napkins, or place mats may be made from any excess fabrics or trims.

If you choose a print fabric that requires matching between panels, you will need to purchase extra fabric. To determine how much extra fabric you will need, measure the design repeat of the fabric and multiply by the number of panels needed for the project. For example, if the design repeat is 18" and you need three panels, multiply 18" by 3. You will need to purchase 54" or 1½ yds of **extra** fabric.

If you need to piece several panels of print fabric and you wish to match the print at the seams, be aware that although many fabrics automatically match from panel to panel at the inside edge of the selvage (**Fig. 1**), others do not (**Fig. 2**). If yours does not, you will need to purchase extra fabric because the "usable width" of the fabric is less than the actual width.

Fig. 1

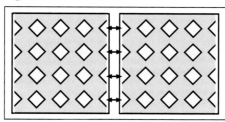

Fig. 2

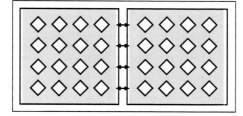

Remember that when print fabrics are pleated or gathered, matching the print is not as critical. So, depending on your project, you may not need to match your print fabric.

MEASURING

When measuring windows, tables, or beds, always use a metal measuring tape; fabric tapes can sag or stretch.

MEASURING WINDOWS

Measure each window individually; windows may look the same but have slightly different measurements.

Refer to **Diagram A** to measure windows for different types of installation (inside or outside) and lengths (sill length, apron length, floor length) of window treatments. Mount curtain rod before measuring for length of window treatment.

To allow bottom or side clearance for window treatments that are sill length, floor length, or that must fit exactly inside a window frame, subtract approx. ½" from length or width measurement before adding measurement indicated in project instructions for headers, casings, hems, etc.

MEASURING TABLES

Refer to **Diagram B** to measure round tables for table skirts. Width or diameter of fabric piece should be diameter of tabletop, plus twice the drop length, plus twice the width needed for hem or edge treatment.

MEASURING BEDS

Refer to **Diagram C** to measure beds for bedspreads or dust ruffles.

DIAGRAM A

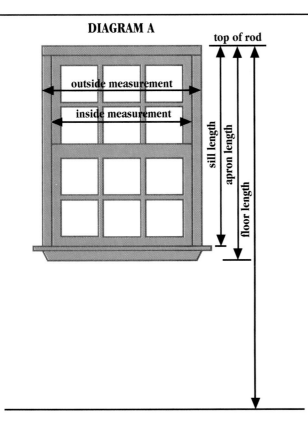

top of rod

outside measurement

inside measurement

sill length

apron length

floor length

DIAGRAM B

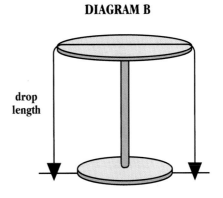

drop length

DIAGRAM C

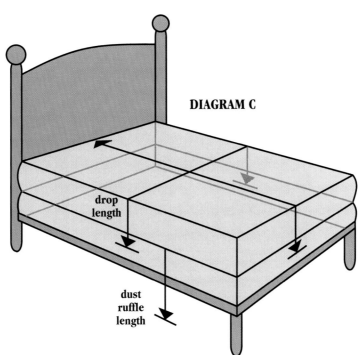

drop length

dust ruffle length

Continued on page 122

FABRICS

SELECTING FABRICS

Many fabrics are suitable for no-sew projects, but light to medium weight cottons work best. If cotton blends are used, pay attention to the content. Some blends may require a lower temperature for ironing, which could cause insufficient melting of the fusible web used, and as a result, cause seams to come apart easily.

Decorator fabrics cost more than fashion fabrics, but are often worth the investment because they provide ease of use during project construction and higher quality and better appearance in the finished project.

Before beginning your project, test the fusible products you will be using on scraps of your chosen fabrics and trims. Increased ironing time may be required when layering fabrics or trims or when using heavier fabrics. Some fabrics shrink when pressed at high temperatures — especially when using steam. If this occurs with your fabric sample and a lower temperature is not sufficient to properly melt the fusible web, choose a different fabric.

Unless the project will be laundered, do not pre-wash fabrics before using them in projects; washing will remove protective finishes which repel soiling.

If a project will require laundering, make sure laundering instructions are similar on all chosen fabrics, trims, and fusible products before purchasing them.

USING SHEETS

Sheets can provide a cost-effective and practical substitute for fabric by the yard in home decor projects. For larger projects, sheets can provide sufficient fabric width to eliminate the need for piecing. For convenience, prefinished hems can often be used as project hems.

Although sheet sizes are "standardized," actual sizes may vary due to differences in hems and trims. You should not only check the size listed on the package, but also measure sheets before cutting.

Unless the project will be laundered, do not pre-wash sheets before using them in projects; washing will remove protective finishes which repel soiling.

COFFEE-DYEING

Some of the fabrics and trims used in this book have been coffee-dyed. To coffee-dye, use 1 tablespoon instant coffee for each cup of hot water used. Dissolve coffee in water; allow to cool. Soak fabric or trims in coffee for several minutes; remove from coffee, allow to dry, and press.

CUTTING FABRIC

First, read through project instructions and plan all cutting. Press fabric before beginning to cut. Use a T-square or carpenter's square to make sure 1 end of fabric is square (**Fig. 1**). If fabric design is printed slightly off-grain, trim end of fabric along the printed design (**Fig. 2**), then square off selvage edge of fabric. If the design is printed visibly off-grain, return the fabric to the store and purchase better fabric.

Fig. 1

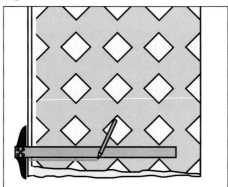

Fig. 2

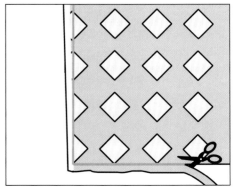

After end of fabric has been squared, carefully measure fabric and mark cutting lines using a disappearing ink fabric marking pen or a fabric marking pencil. Cut fabric carefully using a rotary cutter or sharp shears.

For print fabrics that require matching and piecing, plan cutting very carefully, using the first cut panel as a template for remaining panels (**Fig. 3**).

Fig. 3

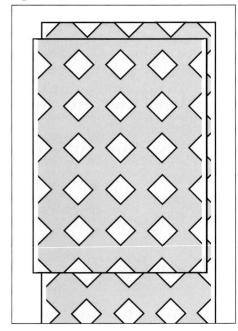

PREPARING A WORK SURFACE

We recommend using a piece of muslin or scrap cotton fabric to protect ironing board from stray fusible adhesives.

For projects which require fusing but are too large to easily handle on an ironing board, prepare an ironing surface on a large table or on the floor. To do this, lay a blanket or comforter on the desired work surface, and then cover the comforter with muslin or scrap cotton fabric.

If the fusible products you use do not recommend using a pressing cloth, you may wish to use a piece of muslin or scrap cotton fabric anyway to protect your iron. It may also be helpful to keep iron cleaner handy for occasional accidents.

FUSING

Instructions for fusing and recommendations for laundering vary widely among fusible products. We recommend that for each project you use only fusible products with similar fusing and laundering instructions.

To use any fusible product, follow the manufacturer's instructions carefully, otherwise an insufficient bond may result.

Always test the fusible product(s) you are using on a piece of scrap fabric before making the project, testing the bond and adjusting conditions as recommended by the manufacturer(s).

If the fusible product you are using does not give satisfactory results with the fabrics or trims you have chosen, try a different fusible product or a different fabric or trim.

For heavier fabrics, you may want to double the amount of web tape used to assemble the project. To do this, fuse web tape to both surfaces to be fused together, remove paper backing, and then fuse as usual.

Web tape can be used to make non-fusible shirring tapes fusible. To do this, fuse web tape along edges and between cords on wrong side of shirring tape, remove paper backing, and fuse in place.

FUSING TECHNIQUES

PIECING FABRIC STRIPS
Note: Use this technique to piece short strips of fabric together to form a longer strip for items such as fabric trim, binding, or welting.

1. To piece 2 fabric strips together, fuse web tape along 1 end on right side of 1 fabric strip. For heavy fabrics, repeat for second fabric strip. Remove paper backing.
2. Matching ends to be joined, place fabric strips right sides together. Fuse ends together. Press seam allowance to 1 side.

PIECING FABRIC PANELS
Note: Use this technique to piece large panels of fabric together to form a larger fabric piece for items such as window treatments, bed coverings, or table skirts.

When piecing fabric panels, you will almost always need to use a full width of fabric at the center of a larger panel with half-widths fused to each side edge to achieve the desired width (**Fig. 1**). This prevents having a seam at the center of the finished fabric piece.

Fig. 1

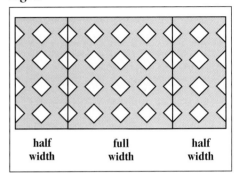

| half width | full width | half width |

When Not Matching Prints:
1. If selvage edges are puckered, trim selvages from fabric panels.
2. Make a single hem (see Making a Single Hem, page 124) along edge of first panel to be joined to second panel. On right side of second panel, fuse web tape along edge to be joined to first panel.
3. Lay panels right side up on a flat surface. Overlap hemmed edge of first panel over taped edge of second panel. Fuse panels together.
4. For heavier fabrics, fuse web tape along wrong side of hemmed edge of first panel before fusing panels together.

Continued on page 124

GENERAL INSTRUCTIONS (Continued)

FUSING TECHNIQUES (Continued)

When Matching Prints:

1. If selvage edges are puckered, clip selvages at 2" to 3" intervals and press.
2. Place panels right sides together, matching selvage edges. Beginning at 1 end of panels, fold top selvage edge back along edges to be joined until pattern on both panels matches (**Fig. 2**); press along fold. Use a fabric marking pen or pencil to mark bottom panel where pattern matches fold of top panel (**Fig. 3**).

Fig. 2

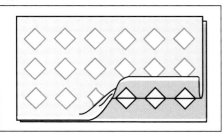

Fig. 3

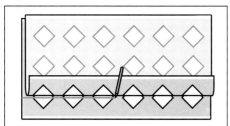

3. For top panel, measure from fold and mark width of web tape along length of excess fabric. Trim fabric along marked line. Unfold edge and make a single hem along edge (see Making a Single Hem, this page).
4. On right side of bottom panel, fuse web tape next to drawn line (**Fig. 4**). Remove paper backing.

Fig. 4

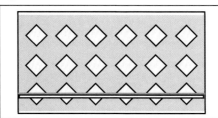

5. Lay panels right side up on a flat surface. Overlap hemmed edge of top panel over taped edge of bottom panel so that design repeats match. Fuse panels together.
6. For heavier fabrics, fuse web tape along wrong side of hemmed edge of top panel before fusing panels together.

MAKING A SINGLE HEM

1. Before hemming a selvage edge that is puckered, clip selvage at 2" to 3" intervals and press.
2. Use web tape width indicated in project instructions (same width as desired hem) and fuse web tape along edge on wrong side of fabric (**Fig. 5**). Do not remove paper backing.

Fig. 5

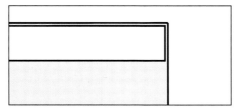

3. Press edge to wrong side along inner edge of tape (**Fig. 6**). Unfold edge and remove paper backing. Refold edge and fuse in place.

Fig. 6

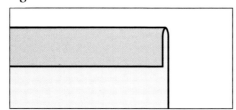

MAKING A DOUBLE HEM

1. Before hemming a selvage edge that is puckered, clip selvage at 2" to 3" intervals and press.
2. Press edge of fabric to wrong side the amount of the desired hem (**Fig. 7**).

Fig. 7

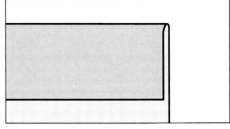

3. Use web tape width indicated in project instructions and fuse web tape along pressed edge (**Fig. 8**). Do not remove paper backing.

Fig. 8

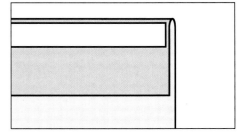

4. Press pressed edge of fabric to wrong side the same amount again (**Fig. 9**). Unfold pressed edge and remove paper backing. Refold edge and fuse in place.

Fig. 9

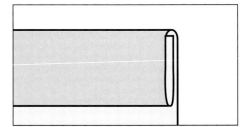

MAKING FABRIC TRIM

Note: Only lightweight fabrics should be used for fabric trim. To give trim flexibility to fit along curved edges, cut fabric strip on the bias.

1. Use web tape width indicated in project instructions and fuse web tape along 1 long edge on wrong side of fabric strip. Do not remove paper backing.

2. Press remaining long edge of fabric to wrong side to meet closest edge of tape (**Fig. 10**). Press taped edge to wrong side along inner edge of tape (**Fig. 11**). Unfold edge and remove paper backing. Refold edge and fuse in place.

Fig. 10

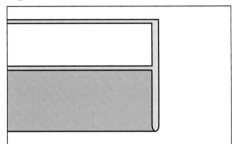

Fig. 11

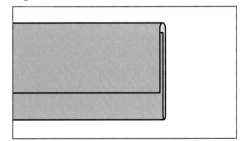

To make any width of fabric trim: Use web tape that is the next smaller width than desired finished width of trim. For example, to make 1 1/4"w fabric trim, use 1"w web tape. To determine width of fabric strip needed, multiply the desired finished width by 2 and add the width of web tape used plus 1/8" for folds. For 1 1/4"w fabric trim, use a 3 5/8"w fabric strip:

$$1\tfrac{1}{4}" \times 2 = 2\tfrac{1}{2}"$$
$$2\tfrac{1}{2}" + 1" + \tfrac{1}{8}" = 3\tfrac{5}{8}"$$

MAKING BINDING

Note: To give binding flexibility to fit around corners and curved edges, cut fabric strip on the bias.

1. With wrong sides together, press fabric strip in half lengthwise; unfold. With wrong sides together, press long raw edges to center.

2. Use the web tape width indicated in project instructions and fuse web tape along each pressed edge on wrong side of binding (**Fig. 12**). Do not remove paper backing.

Fig. 12

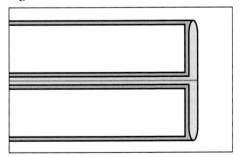

3. Press binding in half lengthwise again. Unfold binding and remove paper backing. Refold binding.

To make any width of binding: Use web tape that is the same width as or next smaller width than desired finished width of binding. For example, to make 1/2"w binding, use 1/2"w or 3/8"w web tape. To determine width of fabric strip needed, multiply the desired finished width by 4 and add 1/8" for folds. For 1/2"w binding, use a 2 1/8"w fabric strip:

$$\tfrac{1}{2}" \times 4 = 2"$$
$$2" + \tfrac{1}{8}" = 2\tfrac{1}{8}"$$

MAKING WELTING

Note: To give welting flexibility to fit along corners and curved edges, cut fabric strip on the bias.

1. Use web tape width indicated in project instructions and fuse web tape along both long edges on wrong side of fabric strip. Remove paper backing.

2. Center cotton cord lengthwise on wrong side of fabric strip.

3. Matching long edges, fold strip over cord; fusing entire width of web tape, fuse edges together.

To make any dia. of welting: Use web tape that is the same width as the desired seam allowance. For example, to make 3/4" dia. welting with a 1/2" seam allowance, use 3/4" dia. cord and 1/2"w web tape. To determine width of fabric strip needed, measure around cord (circumference) and add twice the width of the web tape to the determined measurement. For 3/4" dia. welting with a 1/2" seam allowance, use a 3 3/8"w fabric strip:

$$\text{circumference is approx. } 2\tfrac{3}{8}"$$
$$2\tfrac{3}{8}" + \tfrac{1}{2}" + \tfrac{1}{2}" = 3\tfrac{3}{8}"$$

Continued on page 126

FUSING TECHNIQUES (Continued)

MAKING WIRED FABRIC RIBBON

1. Use web tape width indicated in project instructions and fuse 1 length of web tape along 1 long edge on wrong side of fabric strip. Do not remove paper backing. Press edge of fabric to wrong side along inner edge of tape. Unfold edge and remove paper backing.

2. Cut 1 length of wire 2" longer than fabric strip; straighten wire. Center wire along inner edge of tape on wrong side of fabric strip; bend each end of wire away from center of fabric strip (**Fig. 13**).

Fig. 13

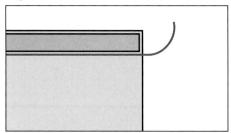

3. Working from 1 end of fabric strip to the other, refold edge of fabric to wrong side over wire and use tip of iron to lightly "tack" edge of fabric in place. Using tip of iron to push wire into fold of fabric, fuse edge of fabric in place. Trim excess wire.

4. Repeat Steps 1 - 3 for remaining long edge of fabric strip.

MAKING A WIRED RIBBON BOW

1. Cut 6" from ribbon for bow center; set aside.

2. Use a pencil to mark center of remaining ribbon length.

3. Measure from 1 end of ribbon the length of 1 streamer; gather ribbon between fingers at this point (**Fig. 14**). Keeping right side of ribbon to the outside, make first loop by matching gathered point to center of ribbon length; gather center also and hold between fingers (**Fig. 15**). Repeat with remaining end of ribbon for second loop and streamer (**Fig. 16**). Wrap center of bow tightly with wire. Trim wire ends close to bow.

Fig. 14

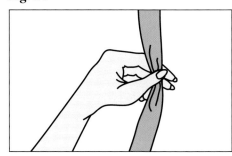

Fig. 15

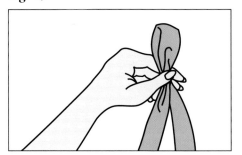

Fig. 16

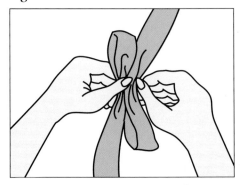

4. For bow center, loosely gather 6" length of ribbon lengthwise. With right side out, wrap gathered ribbon around center of bow, overlapping ends at back and trimming excess. Glue to secure.

5. Trim bow streamers.

To make any size of wired ribbon bow: Determine length of ribbon needed by adding together twice the desired bow width and twice the desired streamer length, plus 6" for bow center. For example, for a 10" wide bow with 12" long streamers, you will need a 50" length of wired ribbon:

$$10" \times 2 = 20"$$
$$12" \times 2 = 24"$$
$$20" + 24" + 6" = 50"$$

MAKING A PILLOW

1. Use web tape width indicated in project instructions and fuse web tape along all edges on right side of pillow back fabric piece. For heavy fabrics, repeat for pillow front fabric piece. Remove paper backing.
2. Place pillow front and back fabric pieces right sides together. Leaving an unfused opening for turning and stuffing along 1 edge, fuse edges of fabric pieces together.
3. Do not clip seam allowances at corners. Turn pillow right side out and carefully push corners outward, making sure seam allowances lie flat. Being careful not to fuse opening, press pillow.
4. Stuff pillow lightly with fiberfill.
5. Placing pins close to opening but not through web tape, pin opening edges together; fuse edges together.

OTHER TECHNIQUES

COVERING LAMPSHADE WITH FABRIC

1. To make pattern, find seamline of lampshade. If shade does not have a seamline, use a pencil to draw a straight line from top edge to bottom edge of shade (**Fig. 1**).

Fig. 1

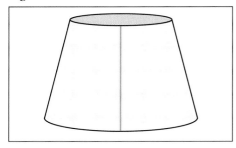

2. With tissue paper extending to right of shade seamline, match 1 edge of paper to seamline; use removable tape to tape in place. Allowing paper to overlap at seamline, wrap paper snugly around shade; tape in place (**Fig. 2**).

Fig. 2

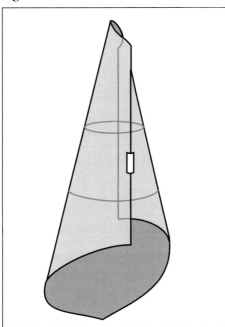

3. Use a pen to mark along top and bottom edges of shade on paper. For overlap at seamline, draw a line on paper from top edge to bottom edge of shade 1" to the right of seamline. Remove paper from shade and cut out pattern along drawn lines.
4. Use pattern to cut shape from fabric.
5. Fold 1 straight edge of fabric 1/2" to wrong side; press in place.
6. Matching unpressed straight edge of fabric to shade seamline, use spray adhesive to glue fabric to shade. Use fabric glue to glue pressed edge in place; allow to dry.

STENCILING

1. For stencil, center acetate over pattern and use permanent felt-tip pen to trace pattern. Place acetate on cutting mat and use craft knife to cut out stencil, making sure edges are smooth.
2. Place item to be stenciled on a protected work surface or place a piece of cardboard covered with waxed paper under area to be stenciled.
3. Hold or use removable tape to tape stencil in place on fabric. Use a clean, dry stencil brush for each color of paint. Dip brush in paint and remove excess on a paper towel. Brush should be almost dry to produce good results. Beginning at edge of cutout area, apply paint in a stamping motion. If desired, shade design by stamping additional paint around edge of cutout area. Carefully remove stencil and allow paint to dry.

CLEANING FINISHED PROJECTS

To clean your project, follow the manufacturer's instructions for the fusible product(s), fabrics, and trims you have used.

If washing or dry cleaning is not recommended, we suggest occasional light vacuuming or tumbling in the dryer on "no heat" setting.

If projects which use shirring tape will be laundered, untie cords and stretch shirred area flat before laundering when possible.

To protect projects from soiling, you may consider using a protective spray finish such as Scotchgard™. If so, remember to test it on scraps from the fabrics and trims used in the project first.

CREDITS

We want to extend a warm *thank you* to the generous people who allowed us to photograph our projects in their homes:

- *Country West:* John and Anne Childs
- *American Country:* Nancy Gunn Porter
- *Romancing the Past:* Dan and Sandra Cook
- *French Country Charm:* Shirley Held
- *Casual Mix:* Carol Clawson

To Magna IV Color Imaging of Little Rock, Arkansas, we say thank you for the superb color reproduction and excellent pre-press preparation.

We especially want to thank photographers Ken West and Larry Pennington of Peerless Photography, and Jerry R. Davis of Jerry Davis Photography, all of Little Rock, Arkansas, for their time, patience, and excellent work.

A special word of thanks goes to the following individuals and businesses in Little Rock, Arkansas, who contributed some of the accessories shown in our photographs:

- Bath and Kitchen Gallery: Windsor pedestal sink with brass fixtures, page 67
- The Bombay Company: 19th-century Trafalgar armchair, page 7; banquet table and Biedermeier console, page 8; composer's bench, page 11; gold-leaf vanity mirror, Tea Poy jewelry box, and brass carriage clock, page 64; braided brass clock, page 66; Ricado oval mirror and Queen Anne bench, page 67; golf prints, page 105; desk, clock, and letter opener, page 107; and leather hat box used as planter, page 109
- Designer Lighting and Accents: Brass Steiffel lamp, page 9
- Ethan Allen: Rice-carved four-poster bed, bed steps, and queen-size mattress and box springs, page 63
- Expressions Custom Furniture: Oversized canvas chair, page 10, and urn with stand, page 11
- Hadidi Oriental Rug Company, Inc.: Black Chinese needlepoint rug, page 7, and ivory wool hooked rug, page 63
- Haverty Furniture Company: 4' and 6' Riverside bookcases, page 109
- Nancy Gunn Porter: Burgundy leather chair, page 109
- The Santa Fe Trading Company: Twig bed, mattress, and leather pouch, page 25; cow skull, page 26; and ladder, page 26
- Allen Trimble: Cowboy boots, page 25, and Western saddle, page 26

We extend a sincere *thank you* to the people who assisted in making and testing the projects in this book: Jennie Black, Lynette Cook, Gazelle Mode, Debra Smith, Karen Tyler, and Dee Ann Younger.